A BLACK MAN IN THE WHITE HOUSE

Barack Obama and the Triggering of America's Racial-Aversion Crisis

CORNELL BELCHER

UPTOWN
PROFESSIONAL
PRESS

Thank you John and Irene Belcher
for being the best parents in the world.

An Uptown Professional Press Book
Published by Water Street Press
Healdsburg, California

Water Street Press paperback edition published October 2016

Designer Credits
Cover art by Sally Eckhoff
Interior design by Typeflow

Produced in the USA

Library of Congress Control Number: 2016955496

ISBN 978-1-62134-360-8

The problem of the twentieth century is
the problem of the color line.

W. E. B. DuBois
The Souls of Black Folk

Contents

Foreword

When I became Chairman of the Democratic National Committee in 2005, we implemented a program that became known as the 50-State Strategy. The idea was to build the party for the long-term by winning incremental elections through registering voters, and recruiting and nurturing candidates at the state and local levels towards future bids for higher office—and to do it by including states in which Republicans had long dominated. Our research and my gut told me that while Democrats weren't losing on the issues, in order to expand the playing field we had to do a better job of competing where it matters most with voters—we had to win with our values. We had to focus on values. Not all of my colleagues bought into that vision, and there was certainly more than one discussion about continuing along the path the party had walked for so long, which was to stick to targeting states where the voters were already friendly.

The 50-State Strategy, however, paid off in what was an historic mid-term election in 2006, with Democrats retaking both the House of Representatives and the Senate, and it was foundational in 2008, helping Barack Obama compete in states long thought of as red states where we shouldn't spend resources—like North Carolina, Nevada and Virginia.

Cornell Belcher was a pollster for the DNC during my tenure as Chairman. When we think about political polling, what often leaps to mind is the science of predicting election results based on feedback from registered voters, and likely voters, and those exiting the voting booth. But the horse-race aspect of polling is really the least important—and least interesting—part of what polls can tell us. Polls show us what Americans think about a wide variety of issues—what they're concerned about, what's most important to them, how policy can be better shaped to improve their lives and the lives of their families. But most importantly, good polling helps us understand the prism of values most Americans use to make sense of their world.

Polling is the useful tool of social science seeking to bring about positive change in people's lives, and while Cornell and I worked together at the DNC he conducted some of the best polling I've ever seen—polling that empowered our understanding of America's changing demographics and the hope that rested within this change for the future of not just the Democratic Party, but the progressive policies it embodies, and the positive changes that can occur when such policies are put into place, rooted in the expressed values of the American people.

Let me be clear: we have at our fingertips a trove of empirical data that proves progressive policies, such as increasing taxes on the wealthiest among us, indeed lead to positive outcomes. A quick look at two cases—the state of Kansas and the state of California—provides a telling overview.

Kansas, functioning under the extremely conservative policies of Governor Sam Brownback, has become an economic wasteland. Domestic spending was slashed in that state and unfunded tax cuts for the rich and for corporations were enacted. The result is that economic growth was halted, job creation came to a standstill, and the state is posting deficits that will likely reach over a billion dollars before all is said and done.

California, on the other hand, did the exact opposite. Under Democratic Governor Jerry Brown, the wholly Democratic majority in the legislature was able to reverse the economic devastation that the previous Republican administration had left behind. The new Democratic majority moved forward with progressive policies based on our progressive values, including a substantial tax increase for the wealthy and increases in spending for education, infrastructure and other domestic programs. In June of 2016, California surpassed France to become the sixth largest economy in the world.°

You read that right: California, one of our fifty states, has become, by itself and under a progressive governor who leads a progressive state legislature, the sixth largest economy in the world.

But, you might say, wait a minute: we have a Democratic president—why isn't the whole country doing as well under his leadership as the state of California is doing under a Democrat?

I propose that a huge chunk of the problem, if not the entirety of it, is due to obstructionist Republicans in Congress who have spent the last eight years doing everything in their power *not* to move the country forward but rather to make sure that President Obama was *unable* to move the country forward. They were guided by their obsession to make sure that the nation's first Black president must fail.

And why did the Republicans stand in President Obama's way? As Cornell makes clear in the pages of this book, the greatest chunk of that problem is that President Obama is Black. The triumph of this country's having at long last elected its first Black chief executive has been met with a backlash of racial aversion so fierce that it has led, just eight years later, to the elevation of an overt racist as the Republican nominee for president.

My friend Cornell Belcher has long been at the vanguard of demographic trends among the emerging younger and browner American voting population. His research allowed us to cut through Beltway criticism back in the early 2000s to learn how to challenge our opponents on what had been, at one point, completely their turf.

Now Cornell has conducted a truly cutting-edge study into racial aversion in our country. What he's found pokes a giant hole through the trope that America is a "post-racial" nation and that our current polarization is simply partisan. His analysis of his data, laid out clearly in the pages that follow, offers us often hard-to-hear insight and understanding into the depth and scope of the racial problems we Americans face today. Hearing hard truths, however, is pretty much the only way we can start to fix any problem. Cornell's work is critical to understanding the path we'll need to walk to reach racial reconciliation in America, but that reconciliation will be crucial for us to win the future.

Governor Howard Dean
September 2016

Author's Note

Over one hundred years ago, W.E.B. DuBois led a campaign that demanded newspaper editors change their style policies and begin to capitalize the "n" in the word Negro. In his opinion, use of the lower case "n" was disrespectful—a sign of overt racism. The apocryphal story of the Georgia newspaper editor who demurred on the grounds that capitalizing the "n" might lead to equality of the races proved DuBois's point. In 1930, however, one of the most important newspapers of the day, the *New York Times*, announced a change in its style policy: "In our 'style book' 'Negro' is now added to the list of words to be capitalized. It is not merely a typographical change; it is an act of recognition of racial self-respect for those who have been for generations in 'the lower case.'"

More recently, Supreme Court Justice Thurgood Marshall advocated, on the same grounds, for the capitalization of the "b" in the word Black when used to reference ethnicity. While some style books do use the capital "b", this is generally the standard only among publications such as *Essence*, *Ebony*, and *Uptown*—that is, publications that target a Black readership. There is not yet a consensus on this matter among the mainstream media. I, however, bow to the wisdom and follow in the tradition of DuBois and Marshall and, in these pages, use B.

Introduction:
A Catastrophic Moment

October 16, 1901

On October 16, 1901, President Theodore Roosevelt sent an invitation to a great American orator, author, and educator to be his guest at dinner. The invitation wasn't unusual; the President and his family were fond of dinner parties and had one nearly every night in the closing months of 1901. But this invitation was something unique: it was issued to Booker T. Washington, a Black man, whose book, *Up From Slavery*, was a popular read at the time. Roosevelt had some hesitance about being the first President to entertain a Black man in the White House; while the likes of Frederick Douglass and Sojourner Truth had consulted with President Lincoln, Booker T. Washington would be the first Black invited to actually sit, in a very social and personable way, at the president's table, with his wife and children. Yes, Roosevelt had the audacity to entertain a Black man as just that—a man—at his White House dinner table.

Washington's first visit with Roosevelt, on September 29, 1901, had been in secret. One of the main topics of discussion between these two venerable, cagey men on that secret evening was the patronage system—a president's prerogative to appoint postmasters, tax assessors, federal judges and the like. Roosevelt had made it clear to Washington that it was his intent to appoint the best men to these jobs (appointing women was not really an issue at the time), regardless of race or—as importantly as it would turn out—party affiliation. He also let it be known that he was willing to appoint Blacks to these sorts of positions when, through attrition, they opened up above the Mason-Dixon line. This was radical at the time, because while Blacks had been appointed to these positions in the South, none yet held such office in the North. Washington was an inscrutable man, but privately he was impressed with what he saw as Roosevelt's enlightenment.

Just days later, Washington had the opportunity to test the President's intent. A federal district court judge in Montgomery, Alabama, died, and Roosevelt would need to replace him. Washington immediately sent his recommendation to the White House: Thomas G. Jones, a former governor of the state, a white man—and a Democrat. In spite of real pushback from other Republicans in his Cabinet, Roosevelt accepted Washington's recommendation and appointed Jones—and was so handed the first true victory of his young presidency. The appointment was met by the public with happy, bipartisan approval—Democrats were pleased, of course, and Republican members of the Grand Old Party (the GOP), knowing that healing the rift that still existed between North and South was to its long-term benefit, hailed it as an action that, according to Edmund Morris is his exceptional book, *Theodore Rex*, "immensely strengthened [its] real and permanent interests."

The dinner party on October 16, when Washington sat not on a chair in the President's office but on one at his table—a dinner party which guests remember as a "simple, cordial"[1] evening—however, sparked scandal and outrage, especially in the South.

The *Memphis-Scimitar* opined, "The most damnable outrage which has ever been perpetrated by a citizen of the United States was committed by the President, when he invited a nigger to dine with him at the White House..."[2] Yes, that is correct; they characterized it as the most damnable outrage ever perpetrated by a citizen! A U.S. Senator from South Carolina, Benjamin R. Tillman, issued a threat: "The action of President Roosevelt in entertaining that nigger will necessitate our killing a thousand niggers in the South before they will reach their place again."[3] Note what he was saying: the mere act of having a Black man in the White House as a man on his own terms, in his own right, would necessitate widespread terror and violence in order to set things back in order. A Black man in the White House had upset the historical order of things in a way many thought dangerous. Southern men swore they would not vote for Roosevelt in the future election.

Understand, they swore not to vote for Roosevelt now not because he had changed any specific policy stand or was fundamentally different from a policy standpoint because of that dinner, but simply because he dared allow a Black man—not a Black servant, but a Black man as a person of unique interest—into the White House as a guest in a social setting. They asserted that Roosevelt had made it impossible for Southern women "with proper self-respect" to accept future invitations to the White House. They assured Roosevelt he would no longer be welcome in Southern homes. Even in the North, support for the Roosevelt-Washington dinner was lukewarm, demoting Roosevelt's invitation to a mere "indiscretion"— the word of choice in a contemporaneous editorial in the *Springfield Republican*. Roosevelt miscalculated how central race matters were to all matters in this country, transcending politics, culture and commonsense in a way nothing else has ever had the power to do—then or now. Race matters are indeed the overpowering variable in the American political equation; it simply cannot be ignored at any time.

The President's public response to the uproar, "I shall have him to dine just as often as I please," was issued in the face of a flood of hate mail and death threats, to both Roosevelt and Washington. It was also lip service. While the President brooded for months over what he saw as his depressingly immature understanding of the complexity of race relations—and while his heart kept faith with his beliefs, "...of one thing I am sure...the only wise and honorable and Christian thing to do is to treat each black man and each white man strictly on his merits as a man..."[4]— and while he privately did meet with Washington again in an advisory capacity, he never again invited him to sit at his dining table in a purely social setting.

For some, the meal that Roosevelt and Washington shared was a catastrophic moment; it shocked the consciousness of whites. It was simply inconceivable that a nigger would be raised to such a haughty position socially—

or in any other way—at the center of American economic, cultural, and political power which that gray-white Virginia freestone-constructed mansion on Pennsylvania Avenue symbolizes. A Black man in the White House threatened to shatter the order of things. A Black man in that most sacred of American buildings would overthrow and ruin the set order of things, presenting a real threat to white privilege. The President of the United States had entertained a Black man as a social equal and, to some, it was a sin that made everything else regarding the President irrelevant. This Black man in the White House represented a threatening first chip in the ruling white-male monolith—and their desperate outcry to take their country back from what they perceived as a dangerous precipice cowed even so courageous and strenuous a man as Theodore Roosevelt. Such was—and is—the power of race matters. Such is the power of the staining image of a Black man in the White House to the white ruling order in America.

A Brief History of Power Tools

In 1901 there were one hundred and thirty documented lynchings—down from a high of two hundred and thirty in 1892. Black men were the victims in one hundred and five of them. The Dyer Anti-Lynching Bill, which sought to make lynching illegal, wouldn't be introduced in Congress until 1918.

The etymology of the word "lynch" is in dispute, though

it likely comes to us by way of Charles Lynch, Virginia planter and American Revolutionary who was the head of a county court in that state, and who regularly jailed supporters of the crown during the Revolutionary War. It wasn't within his jurisdiction to pronounce these sentences, and, so, extralegal activity came to be known as lynching.

We commonly understand the word lynching these days to have racial implications, but those didn't attach until nearly a century later, during the Civil War, when abolitionists and others who opposed slavery were the main targets. It was after Reconstruction, after slavery had been abolished in the U.S., however, that lynchings—extralegal punishment imposed by mobs without due process—really ramped up. While slavery was legal, it would have been contrary to the existing Southern social order to summarily execute slaves, because they represented significant economic investment on the part of Southern white elites. But when the slaves were freed, and enfranchised—suddenly the legal equals of poor Southern whites—lynching became the tool of choice for those poor whites to assert their continued dominance and power over Blacks. To keep freed men from getting an education, from going to work, and from exercising their new franchise to vote. To instill fear.

"Americans woke up to a different nation yesterday. In place of old victories built upon the politics of bitterness and division, in place of the old scourge of racial enmity, a new maturity and responsibility had found its majority. Real change is now not so audacious a hope.

"[A]ny American worthy of the name could grasp— regardless of political affiliation—the significance of what had occurred in the election of Barack Obama as the nation's first African-American president."

Editorial, Pittsburgh Post-Gazette
November 6, 2008

"This, this is the beginning of living out [MLK's dream]. It means that a majority of people are beginning to— as I say, they—they chose faith in America over fear about racial differences."

Andrew Young, radio interview on
The Takeaway, *November 5, 2009*

"Fair is foul, and foul is fair
Hover through the fog and filthy air."

Shakespeare,
Macbeth

January 20, 2009

One hundred and eight years after Booker T. Washington's dinner with Theodore Roosevelt at the executive mansion incited racial outrage, America's first Black president took the oath of office, and he and his family took up residence in the most famous house that slaves built. Many commentators took the election results as evidence the country had entered a new "post-racial" era wherein Americans had at last let go of centuries of racial baggage and whole-heartedly embraced equality. Indeed, I was in Paris shortly after the election, talking about American politics, and the French would come up to me and literally congratulate me as an American, for our now being post-racial.

It was as if the election of Obama had shown that America was no longer divided racially, that the racial issue in America had been solved. While a nice thought, it couldn't be further from reality. The changing cultural and racial demographics of the country had, indeed, finally allowed the nation to overcome a monumental electoral political barrier, but it did not exorcise the racial ghost—or, as W. E. B. DuBois would put it, America's central problem. No indeed; that ghost, under clear and present threat, would be unbound now in ways many of us had thought—or hoped—the country had moved on from. That ghoul would now use all its remaining power to delegitimize the Black man in the White House and stop him from effectively governing.

For a portion of the American population, the election of Barack Obama was catastrophic, indeed; a Black man was in the White House and the historic order of things were cast into peril. Most habitual traditions of governing, of respect, of basic rules and moral practices that, despite disagreement, have acted to keep our government functioning through natural disasters, corruption, crime, and wars would be suspended due to the absolute catastrophe to the tribal order that was the presidential election of Barack Obama—a Black man in the White House. The panicked tribal response to a Black man in the White House would overrun the order of the Republican Party, putting them on a path of internal civil war and bringing our political system to a dysfunctional screeching halt. Indeed, no cost—from national default, to government closings, to outright refusing to do the basic legislative duties of Congress such as filling government appointments— would be too great for those raked by catastrophe and thus driven to "take the country back". These blunt calls to "take back the country", and the fears they represent of America losing its way and heading in the wrong direction, are the natural and predictable reactions to this cataclysm— and the nomination of the unrepentant and overt racist Donald Trump as the Republican party's standard bearer in 2016 is the wholly unsurprising upshot of a party that has been race-baiting, albeit covertly, for generations. They have simply come out in the open with the nomination of Trump. A Black man in the White House changes everything.

Lynching has long since been a felony in every state of the Union, but there are new tools that those who do not embrace a "post-racial" America have taken up in the struggle to continue to assert dominance. To keep minorities from voting, to hamstring and discredit a twice-elected president. To nullify a presidency. This book presents stunning new research that illuminates just how deep and jagged are America's racial fault lines as it relates to recent elections. It explains much of what has unfolded politically as a result of the moment so many on the far right view as catastrophic. It also looks to shine a light on the modern-day tools those who fall within those fault lines use in their attempts to mitigate the political event they see as catastrophic, and "take back the country".

THERE IS ANOTHER, larger and more proactive purpose to this book as well. As I write, in the summer of 2016, the contest to elect the successor to Barack Obama has not yet been decided. The choice between the two candidates is a no-brainer for those of us who count diversity as a blessing, human dignity as a family-of-man value, and world peace as a worthwhile goal. It's not so much a battle of ideology as it is fundamentally a battle between those wishing to hold on to the old racial ruling order and those seeking a more perfect union. The polls, as of this writing, both provide opportunity and reinforce dismay: while Hillary Clinton has, on average, led in the national polling, her advantage is not substantial as most white voters continue to back Trump even as he has been rejected by much of the Republican establishment, including the party's last president and presidential nominee. It's as if much of the Republican establishment bought into the bullshit it was

selling and actually thought they were winning solid majorities of white voters, ever since President Johnson signed
the Civil Rights Act, because of the GOP's policy prescrip-
tions. Racial party re-alignment established upon and
because of President Johnson's signing of Civil Rights legislation remains as durable today as ever; the candidacy of
a reality TV star with questionable business practices and
zero public policy experience speaks power to that truth.
We are bearing witness to the truth of American politics—
nothing trumps tribalism. While not the absolute or only
variable, race is by and large the great political organizing
line in America.

Still, whether Donald Trump wins or loses on Election
Day, the mere fact of his candidacy, that he was nominated
as the standard bearer for one of our country's two major
parties, speaks to the urgency of the larger purpose I have
in mind. That's because, win or lose, Donald Trump has,
in one critical way, already won. He has already succeeded
in stripping away the genteel veneer in which bigotry has
been cloaked for decades in our politics. He's refused to
tread gingerly around his prejudices—from sexism[5] to xenophobia[6] to racism,[7] he's put them front and center—and
we've watched, many of us in disbelief and even horror, as
his rants strike a nerve in followers and they flock to him.
He's opened the door to the subbasement of America's psy-
che and exposed to us just how ugly the mess remains after
centuries of refusing to deal with it.

Whether Donald Trump wins the 2016 election remains, for the time being, a question. Perhaps he won't
win at the ballot box but only, as has been hinted, win by

"monetizing"[8] his bid to lead the free world, turning his current "audience" into a ratings bonanza for his own mini media empire.[9] But however he capitalizes on his new-found influence beyond the 2016 election, it's a great favor to us that he's laid the problem out so starkly. His ravings may not be a constructive part of the solution, but we'll be remiss if we don't see them as instructive.

Importantly, then, this book lays out the steps we have to take and the strategies we have to embrace if America is to have any hope of rising above not just this latest mouth-piece for racial enmity, but five hundred years of suffering under it. In order to compete and win the future, America must move on and let go of the historic tribal pecking order that in the most concrete ways helps to pick the winners and losers in our society. This tribal, gamed system will not serve us well in the face of competition from a rising Pacific rim and a struggling but still largely united Europe. To paraphrase DuBois, "The problem of the twenty-first century remains the color line." Contrary to what you may have heard from media types, the election of the nation's first African-American president was in no way a conclusion to the hard conversation Americans need to have about race, and thus power. But it *was* the trigger for the hardest conversation we, as Americans, will ever have. If we can see the term "post-racial" for what it actually is as of 2016—both depressingly immature and cunningly deflective, perhaps the dialogue we really do need to have about race can actually begin and we can move as one people toward a more inclusive and perfect union.

Color in Context

> **"**I'm not for secession, but I understand why people might be.**"**
>
> *Sean Hannity*

> **"**Those who don't know history are doomed to repeat it.**"**
>
> *Edmund Burke*

The (Dis)Loyal Opposition

In order to better understand both the people who experienced the election of Barack Obama as a catastrophic moment and the tools they put to use to undermine his presidency, a little background is helpful. Who are these people? From what place does their worldview emerge? What is it that prompts them to action?

There is no easy, one-size-fits-all answer to these questions. Their attitudes and actions come out of a stew made

up of history, religion, politics, media, culture, and demographics. But let's start with our focus on history. We can
safely say that the deviance begins in a natural, and even
honorable, place: the Loyal Opposition.

By definition, the Loyal Opposition embodies the duty
of the minority party to oppose the party that is in power—
and to do it in a constructive and responsible manner,
rooted in a fundamental loyalty to the government as a
whole. Indeed, the concept of Loyal Opposition is part of
the bedrock of democracy—opposition enhances debate,
deepens thought, allows peaceful and civilized resolution,
and can be a genuine benefit to the laws that result from
the legislative process. It is the mechanism by which legislators can disagree with the policies of a government without seeking to destroy that government itself.

Some readers might look back at recent history and con-
clude that Ronald Reagan was responsible for dealing the
first blow to the integrity of the concept of Loyal Opposition when, in his first inaugural address, he insisted that "...
government is not the solution to our problem, government
is the problem."[10] Who, after all, would not seek to destroy
that thing which is, in and of itself, the problem? Others
might give the credit to Grover Norquist, who famously declared, "I'm not in favor of abolishing the government. I just
want to shrink it down to the size where we can drown it in
the bathtub." In truth, however, "limited government" and
"states' rights" had been long-running themes on the right.[11]
Reagan and Norquist just managed to frame the ideas so
they seemed a fresh way to address then-current events, and
reduce them to the ultimate sound bites.

That said, when did the idea of killing the government gain the sort of traction that allowed Republicans in Congress to nearly drive the country off the cliff by refusing to raise the debt ceiling? When did the word "loyal" get lost among the "opposition"? When did the shit get real?

As it would have gone against the existing social order in the pre-Civil War South to summarily execute slaves who represented, as I pointed out in the Prologue, significant investment on the part of Southern white elites, it wouldn't have been possible to raise the ire of what has become the "Tea Party" base to murderous action with an affable white man like Reagan as president—or even with a white man like Bush, who led the nation blindly into two wars, spilling her blood, spending her treasure, and almost gleefully running up the nation's debt.

But when a Black man was elected president, the gloves came off—and not merely metaphorically. In 2008, the year of Obama's first presidential win, the FBI reported an 8% increase in anti-Black hate crimes—from 2,658 in 2007 to 2,876 in 2008.[12] Some of those hate crimes occurred on Election Day itself. Just hours after the polls closed, three young white men on Staten Island decided, according to a federal indictment, "to find African-Americans to assault"; they found a seventeen-year-old Black teenager and beat him with a metal pipe while they shouted, "Obama!"[13] In Madison County, Idaho—which some claim as the "reddest county" in America, second- and third-graders chanted "Assassinate Obama!" on the bus on their way to school the day after the historic election.[14] In Springfield, Mississippi, in an event unnervingly reminiscent of the violence that has historically been perpetrated upon Black churches—and an unsettling foreshadowing of events that would unfold in June 2015 at the Emanuel African Methodist Episcopal Church in Charleston, South Carolina—a Black church, the Macedonia Church of God in Christ, was torched and burned to the ground following John McCain's concession speech.[15]

Who are the people who teach their children to call for the murder of an elected American president? What forces shape criminals who act out their political losses by beating children and burning down churches—and gunning down church-goers? From whence do the purveyors of such hate emerge?

The (Original) Tea Party

In the same way that presenting government as the problem was not new in 1981, the contemporary "Tea Party" was not a new idea in 2009.

The Boston Tea Party was an iconic American event— the first act in what would become the American Revolution. Considering how the event has been misunderstood by modern-day conservatives who have co-opted its imagery, it will be beneficial to include here a brief outline of what the Boston Tea Party was actually all about.

The shortest possible telling of the event is that on December 16, 1773, the Sons of Liberty staged a political protest wherein they boarded the ships of the East India Company and destroyed an entire shipment of the company's tea by throwing it into Boston Harbor. They did this in response to the Tea Act of May 10, 1773, an Act of the Parliament of Great Britain, which imposed duties on the tea drunk by the residents of its American colonies. "No taxation without representation" was the rallying cry of the colonists.

Unfortunately—apart from some members of the contemporary American "Tea Party" having an affinity for the breeches, frock coats, and tricorne hats that were fashionable in the late 18th century—that seems to be about as much of the story of the Boston Tea Party as the modern-day Right Wing can grasp; the circumstances of the actual event are much more nuanced.

The practice of drinking tea—as well as coffee and hot chocolate—emigrated to the Americas with colonists from both England and the Netherlands, and they drank it not only in their homes. Coffeehouses, modeled after their London counterparts, were powerfully popular at the time—places where colonists gathered and, stimulated by caffeine, distributed news, exchanged ideas, engaged in robust debate. We might think of them as the Starbucks of their time, but these early coffeehouses were in no part as mundane. For one thing, of course, no one was isolated behind a computer screen or plugged into earbuds. Friend or stranger, no matter his socioeconomic status or political leanings, was welcomed into convivial conversations that were often lively—and frequently more than merely lively. The coffee of the era may have been just as the Turkish proverb said, "black as hell, strong as death, sweet as love" (and filled with grit), but sailors and shoeblacks, lawyers, laborers, and landed gentry came together to drink it up and discuss and dissect the daily news. Coffeehouses of the 1700s were incubators for real social change—and the importance of the beverages the colonists drank while they were creating their new society can't be underestimated.

Since the 1760s, the British Crown had been trying to impose a tax on tea consumed in the colonies, first with the Stamp Act of 1765 and then the Townshend Act of 1767—and colonists responded by boycotting British tea, neatly circumventing the taxes and providing for the continuing demand for the product with a hardy smuggling trade. The Tea Act of 1773 was one more in a string of attempts by the British crown to exact the tea tax, although the Act itself imposed no new taxes. It actually involved a *repeal* of taxes.

The purpose of the Tea Act was, in part, to prop up a corporation, the failing British East India Company. To do this, Parliament permitted the company to sell tea from its overstocked warehouses in London directly to the colonies without having to pay the tax that was normally imposed when the company sold through its London offices. Relieved of its obligation to pay its own tax, the company was thus able to pass along the savings to colonial consumers, and thus sell tea more cheaply than the smugglers could manage. Parliament hoped that by undercutting the cost of smuggled tea they would convince the colonists to buy the East India tea. And *then*, with the act of purchasing the taxed tea, Parliament would have the colonists' implicit agreement to its right to impose that tax, as well as others, if it saw fit.

In many colonies, the ships carrying the untaxed tea were successfully turned away from port but, in Massachusetts, Royal Governor Thomas Hutchinson would not allow the ships to be turned away, nor let the tea be returned to England. Parliament reacted to the Tea Party that followed Hutchinson's ruling by trying to punish Massachusetts. On March 28, 1774, they passed the Coercive (or Intolerable) Acts, which, among other things, shut down commerce in Boston and repealed the right to self-government in the entire state.

A little more than a year later, on April 18, 1775, Paul Revere made his famous ride.

SO WE SEE that the tax on tea was not the only issue that outraged the colonists and caused them to revolt against English rule.

In 1763, the British Parliament decided that there needed to be new policies to administer the vast territory west of the American colonies—the territory that had been acquired by Britain from France in the French and Indian War. Though various of the colonies had plans to develop the territory—and all the riches that lay within it—George III issued a proclamation that closed the western territory to settlement by the colonists, thwarting the colonists' plans—and cheating them, the colonists felt—of enormous opportunity.

In 1764 the Parliament of Great Britain passed the Currency Act—which was actually a series of several acts—that banned the payments of English debt with colonially printed paper money. Parliament's intent was to protect British merchants from depreciation in colonial currency, but the effect was to reduce the money supply in the colonies by half, which in turn severely increased the debt of colonial merchants and traders. As a result, unemployment and poverty in the colonies soared and—according to Alexander Hamilton, the fledgling nation's first treasury secretary—the colonists knew exactly whom to blame for their impoverishment: the crown.

In 1765, Parliament passed the Quartering Act, which provided that the colonists were required to house—and feed—ten thousand British troops in public buildings, or, if required, *private* homes. The colonists considered the Quartering Act a tool of oppression—as anyone might who had to provide room and board to a militia that was in residence in order to protect the authority of British-appointed governors who did not have to answer to the colonists for their actions. Indeed, the Quartering Act was one of the main inspirations for the Second Amendment.

As Benjamin Franklin summarized, the American Revolution can be attributed "...to a concurrence of causes: the restraints lately laid on their trade, by which the bringing of foreign gold and silver into the Colonies was prevented; the prohibition of making paper money among themselves, and then demanding a new and heavy tax by stamps; taking away, at the same time, trials by juries, and refusing to receive and hear their humble petitions."[16] The colonies, in other words, did not revolt because of a little tax on their tea.

SO WE SEE the Founding Fathers were not opposed to taxes, per se. Unlike the modern-day citizens of the U.S., who duly elect representatives to the Congress every two years, what the colonists objected to was having no colonial presence in the British Parliament to speak to a variety of their interests far beyond a little tax. To use Revolutionary War imagery as a metaphor for what the contemporary "Tea Party" insists is its concern about taxes is to have a simplistic understanding of American history, if not a thorough misunderstanding of it.

So is there a more apt historical model for the "Tea Party"?

The Founding Fathers were in the process of building an economy, constructing a new social order, writing a constitution, forming a government, *creating a country*. One in which all men were created equal. Notably, this equality did not extend, upon the Founders' inception, beyond white males. Those white males did not include women in the new franchise they were devising, and the majority of them were slaveholders whose vision of parity fell markedly short in matters of race as well. That said, their concept for the new country they were making was radical for the time, a formal if limited throwing off of the social order they knew—the aristocracy, and the monarchy—for a wholly revolutionary experiment with egalitarianism.

In order to arrive at an appropriate model for today's "Tea Party", then, we have to think of a time when a group of malcontents sought not to create but to destroy the country. To quash the economy, cling to an outdated social order, circumvent the Constitution, foment hatred of the established government, and tear the nation apart at the seams.

If you thought of the Confederacy, you're right on target. The similarities between the mindsets of antebellum Southerners and members of the contemporary "Tea Party" are astonishing. They use the same language as a cloak—"states' rights" as a smokescreen for slavery then and racism now; they have the same commitment to disenfranchisement—think modern-day attempts to limit voting rights; they share a Southern Strategy that uses many of the same tactics.

Think I'm being too hard on the "Tea Party"? Think again. During the Civil War, the South attempted to secede from the Union a duly elected president sought to preserve. Today, according to analysis of the White House's "We the People" program, 43% of Republican respondents say they would support a modern-day secession movement.[17]

So, who was it who first twisted history, choosing the wrong war upon which to model his or her movement?

The mythology of the "Tea Party" is that it sprang directly and organically from a rant by CNBC Business News Network editor Rick Santelli on the floor of the Chicago Mercantile Exchange on February 19, 2009. In truth, it is an astroturf effort, curated collaboratively by the tobacco industry and the billionaire Koch brothers, that dates back to the 1980s; their first website, www.usteaparty.com, a URL currently owned by Freedomworks—went live in 2002.[18]

You might say the neo-Tea Partiers got lucky with the election of America's first Black president. Their campaign had been desultory—and mostly unheard-of—until the country elected Barack Obama. Then they really had a meaty something to sink their teeth into. The fact of a Black Chief Executive could be put to good use in rousing the rank-and-file—generating fear along tribal lines. It would be an unholy marriage—this union of corporate interests with the politics of race, but it would be effective.

A Tea Partier by Any Other Name

The Republican Party in the second decade of the 21st century is more Southern, more conservative, older, and whiter than at any other time in history. At the same time, the Republican Party is taking its marching orders from a radical wing of the party that identifies itself as the "Tea Party"—a group that is, again, largely Southern, unabashedly conservative, and nearly 100% white.

Part of the antagonism on the Right is surely a result of the Republican Party throwing a collective temper tantrum because they are out of power. Think back to the obstruction thrown in the way of the last Democratic president who got in their way; Bill Clinton was impeached.

But there is something wholly different about the opposition President Barack Obama faces. There is an edge of hysteria to it. Of irrational rage. Of this opposition being more *personal* than other presidents have had to contend with.

Why is that?

The 2008 election, in which American voters elected their first Black president, was viewed by many as an event that would change America forever, finally ending our long legacy of racial discrimination and antagonism. As the editorial board of the *Pittsburgh Post-Gazette* put it, the election was going to usher in "a new maturity and responsibility"[19] on race relations. *New York Times* columnist Thomas Friedman went so far as to hail the election as one in which we finally closed the book on the Civil War.[20] In the immediate afterglow of the election, the dream of a "post-racial" America that had been discussed so much before the election seemed as though it might be coming true.

At the same time, however, there were indications that Barack Obama's election could have the opposite effect. As soon as Obama clinched the nomination in June 2008, civil rights watchdog organizations cited a dramatic rise in interest in white power groups, causing concern in many quarters.[21] And, indeed, as I have already pointed out, Obama's election was closely followed by an unprecedented rise in hate crimes—such as public displays of nooses, vandalism, and racist graffiti—across the country,[22] and the FBI reported an eight-percent increase in hate-crime attacks on African-Americans from 2007 to 2008.[23] While perhaps on a relatively small scale, fears of a white backlash against Obama's election also seemed to be coming true.

So what has *actually* happened to racial attitudes in America as a result of Obama's campaigns and governing? The immediate response is that they are all over the map.

Levels of racial antagonism have varied significantly over the past six years in response to media hype, rumor, partisan politics and the reality of a Black president. Specifically, among white voters in the typical battleground presidential-election states, attitudes have shifted from a relatively stable status quo during the election season of 2008, to a brief "post-racial" glow following the election, to significant and increasing polarization under the Obama presidency. Rather than bringing Americans together under a new understanding of race and ushering in racial tolerance, the reality of a Black president has exacerbated existing differences in racial attitudes in America. Obama has brought the fear of an end to white political dominance in America to a boiling point.

I set out to analyze the twists and turns in white-battleground America's levels of racial antagonism and tolerance from the general election of 2008 through the reelection of Barack Obama in 2012 but, of course, then had to initiate polling again checking racial aversion to capture the rise of Trump. Through a series of surveys over this time period, I tracked an index of racial antagonism, along with opinions about candidate and President Obama, to show how opinions responded to the political realities of the two elections and the intervening governing period, and how attitudes in turn affected voting in 2008 and 2012.

Not only did overall attitudes change over time, demonstrating heightened levels of negative racial attitudes during the Obama presidency, but individual levels of racial antagonism and opinions of the president varied by party affiliation over time: Democrats became increasingly racially positive over the course of the Obama election and presidency, while independents and, primarily, Republicans became significantly more racially resentful. And while the aggregate level of racial antagonism dropped again after the 2012 election, the partisan racial polarization of attitudes remains and, indeed, jumped astonishingly among Republicans going into 2016, helping to explain Donald Trump now as the nominee for the GOP.

Polarized partisan attitudes are to be expected over the course of a presidency. Bill Clinton certainly felt this over the course of his two terms, as I've already said, and George Bush was just as certainly pushed from the left during his eight years. The polarized racial attitudes we find during Obama's presidency, on the other hand, are a direct response to the President's race and Americans' affective reactions to electing and having a Black man in the White House.

AS MANY BEFORE us have argued, race and racial attitudes are, and have always been, a defining force in American politics. As Carmines and Stimson put it: "The only time that seems a reasonably certain origin for racial controversy in America would be the date the first Black slave was brought ashore...we ought not look for the origin of racial issues in American politics because racial issues predate American politics."[24]

Therefore, long before Barack Obama arrived on the political scene, presidents and presidential contenders have been grappling with America's troubled racial history, and the influence of race in American politics that runs the gamut from individual-level perceptions and preferences to governmental operations and policy. The rise of the first realistic African-American contender for the office, however, brought with it completely new political dimensions to the national stage.

Obama was far from the first Black political candidate to run for election in this country, and not even near the first Black candidate to face a majority white electorate. That said, running as a Black candidate for the office considered the peak of national power and honor in a country with a history of racism brought issues of political discrimination and voter bias to the fore in a way never seen before. To understand the context in which Barack Obama made his presidential run, and thereby begin to understand the attendant ups and downs of racial attitudes in America, it's necessary to review the history of public opinion leading up to that moment. Let's take a look at racial attitudes in the latter half of the 20th century and early part of the 21st century to set the stage for Obama's run.

The (Recent) History of Whites' Racial Attitudes

The role of race in Americans' attitudes and beliefs is, to put it mildly, complicated. Over the past six or seven decades, since the polling industry has been able to gauge opinions scientifically, some previously negative attitudes towards Blacks have become significantly more positive, while others have not. In some areas, while the American public professes a desire for positive racial goals, such as racial equality and supporting a Black president, they hold at the same time attitudes that would seem to undermine such achievements. Many like the idea of an African-American being able to rise to the highest of heights in America, but they simultaneously hold views of African-Americans that stand as a hurdle to that accomplishment.

By most outward appearances, whites in America have become much more accepting of Blacks, both personally and in politics. Not only do whites have significantly more positive attitudes towards Blacks as a group than they used to, they also profess a nearly unanimous willingness to vote for a hypothetical Black president—statistics often cited as evidence that race played a minor role in the 2008 election.

The American National Election Studies (ANES), the long-running standard for in-depth political surveys in America, has been measuring whites' attitudes towards Blacks since the 1950s. Starting in 1964, the ANES has consistently been asking its respondents how they feel towards Blacks as a group, using a "feeling thermometer" which ranges from 0 to 100. Respondents place groups at the specific temperature on the 100-point scale that reflects how they feel towards the group, with 0 being very cold and 100 being very warm. Since this question was instituted about Blacks (actually called "Negroes" up until 1972), the results show whites' affect towards Blacks becoming increasingly positive. In 1964 whites rated Blacks an average of just above 60 degrees. In 2004 (the most recent survey for which data are available at this writing) the rating had increased almost 10 degrees to just under 70—a significant improvement.

Perhaps even more impressive is the change in white Americans' attitudes towards African-Americans as political leaders. The public has gone from an aggregate unwillingness to support a Black candidate for president to almost unanimous willingness to do so—in theory.

Since 1958, Gallup and other pollsters have been asking Americans the same basic question about support for a hypothetical Black candidate for president. Gallup's question typically reads: "If your party nominated a generally well-qualified man for President and he happened to be a Black, would you vote for him?"[25] When the question was first asked in 1958, fewer than 40% of all Americans said they would vote for their own party nominee if he were Black.

Attitudes changed quickly, however. By 1968 more than 60% of Americans said they would vote for a Black nominee from their party. By the year 2000, attitudes had done a complete reversal from fifty years earlier—from unwillingness to support a Black candidate to virtual unanimity of support. By the 21st century, support for a Black party nominee in the general election was solidly in the 90 - 95% range, and remains at that level, at least through this writing. While these numbers are among all Americans, attitudes among whites are no different. In the December 2007 Gallup Poll (the most recent included in *Fig. 1*), the proportion of whites reporting that they would support a Black president was the same as the proportion of all adults—93%.

Fig. 1.   Whites' Willingess to Support a Black Presidential
Candidate

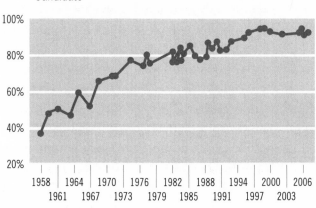

From these easy measures it is obvious that attitudes towards Blacks have changed, both socially and politically. And if these numbers told the whole story, we could indeed wash our hands of the problems of racism and discrimination. These measures do not, however, provide the full story of whites' attitudes towards Blacks in America today. While things have certainly improved, dramatically even, when one looks below the surface the view gets murkier.

As I've already noted, racial attitudes are complicated, and not easily explained by a few attitude questions. In fact, we do not have to go much further or deeper than the questions above in order to find that negative racial attitudes remain a substantial problem, despite five decades of positive changes in attitudes. First, while white Americans' views of Blacks have improved significantly over time, as measured by the ANES, their views of themselves as a group—whites—have always been significantly higher than their ratings of Blacks, and they remain so today.

Over the past forty years, whites' views of Blacks have improved significantly, and their views of whites have decreased significantly on the feeling thermometer score—indicating a reduction in group differences and perhaps racial group identity among whites vis-à-vis Blacks. In 1964 the average difference in whites' ratings of Blacks and whites was twenty-five points—a full quarter of the thermometer measure. By 2004 this discrepancy had been cut to roughly 4.5 points—a stunning change.

At the same time, however, whites' warmth towards their own racial group remains statistically significantly higher than their warmth towards Blacks, making it clear that whites do still distinguish between themselves and Blacks as a group. This result holds true not only for general affective attitudes, but also for more specific issues and situations.

One major reason for this distinction is that whites feel that Blacks are simply different from themselves. Specifically, in a *Newsweek* survey released in May 2008, only 30% of white Americans feel they have "a lot" in common with Blacks in their social class. Just about half of white Americans feel they have "some" common interests with similarly situated African-Americans. In other words, even when equalizing class differences, whites do not feel akin to Blacks.

A particularly touchy subject—interracial marriage—shows the same core of discomfort on the part of whites. In the abstract whites are extremely supportive of Blacks as equals, but they become less magnanimous when the issues touch closer to home. According to that same *Newsweek* survey of May 2008, 71% of white Americans said they approve of marriage between Blacks and whites. But when the question loses its abstraction and becomes about white Americans' daughters dating (not marrying) a Black man, just 60% of whites said they would be "OK" with it. Just over a third of whites would be upset about it.

These personal or social views of Blacks are not, of course, the only complicated part of race relations in America—political attitudes are as well. While over 90% report that they themselves would be willing to vote for a Black nominee from their own party, they show substantial skepticism that their fellow Americans would be willing to do the same.

According to a CBS News survey in March of 2008, 93% of whites nationally said that whether a candidate was white or Black would make no difference to *their own* vote. At the same time, however, only 55% believe that most of the people they know would be willing to vote for a Black candidate. In other words, virtually all white Americans profess to be equally as willing to vote for a Black candidate as a white candidate, but doubt the intentions of others. This presents an interesting puzzle. If both questions are taken as measures of true attitudes, then white Americans are grossly misinformed about the preferences of their friends and acquaintances. An alternative explanation is that some respondents are not answering the question of their own willingness to vote for a Black president with complete veracity. Indeed, I read that, fairly or not, to mean only just about half of white Americans are actually open to voting for a Black candidate.

Academic research into negative racial attitudes demonstrates that the reluctance whites report on behalf of others to support a Black candidate actually reflects hesitation within themselves. Direct survey questions to a respondent about politically sensitive issues can often result in respondents reporting what they think is correct to say, rather than what they truly feel. Questions about what "others" would do, on the other hand, are easier for respondents to answer in terms of their own attitudes should they hold negative, and possibly politically incorrect attitudes.

In a similar vein, in that same CBS News survey, while reporting willingness on their own part to support a Black nominee from their own party, substantial portions of white America also feel that the country as a whole is not actually *ready* for a Black president. For example, 64% of Americans said they thought the U.S. was "ready" for a Black president in the same survey in which 93% said race made no difference to their vote. Here again we find whites saying that they themselves are fine, and even supportive, of the idea of a Black president, but that, in their judgment, others are not.

While it is not possible to quantify exactly the proportion of white Americans that may be responding "correctly" to the question of supporting a Black nominee, rather than truthfully, it is clear that there is hesitation among white Americans to support a Black candidate for president. Again, attitudes are more complicated than some measures lead us to believe.

Another important area of whites' attitudes towards Blacks involves stereotypical beliefs about them. In the preceding paragraphs I've talked about mostly affective views of Blacks—positive or negative attitudes towards them. Stereotyping involves judgments of the content of Blacks' character or beliefs, and these judgments have typically focused on perceived lack of effort and ability on the part of Blacks in America.

Historically whites have held a host of negative stereotypes of Blacks, focusing on the perceived inferiority of Blacks on multiple characteristics.[26] For example, Blacks have traditionally been seen as less intelligent than whites, less industrious, and more violent. Further undermining the idea that attitudes towards Blacks have improved, even given the affect measure's stunning increase, is solid evidence that these stereotypes persist to this day.

Color by Numbers

> **"**The next half century marks key points in continuing trends—the U.S. will become a plurality nation, where the non-Hispanic white population remains the largest single group, but no group is in the majority."[27]

Thomas L. Mesenbourg
U.S. Census Bureau Acting Director
December 12, 2012

> **"**...50.4 percent of our nation's population younger than age 1 were minorities as of July 1, 2011."[28]

U. S. Census Bureau Report
May 17, 2012

These attitudes don't flourish in a vacuum. As I have already noted, they flow from a concoction of history, religion, politics, media, culture, and demographics. As Winston Churchill told us, in a statement as true as any statesman has ever uttered, "History is written by the victors." That is, those who win—who are in power, who make up the majority—get to tell the story. And there simply isn't any question at all that the history of America through its almost two hundred and fifty years of existence has been written by the white elites who have held power in all that time. As much as the United States entertains the notion of itself as a "melting pot"—a place where Emma Lazarus's huddled masses yearning to breathe free are welcomed to come together from various heterogeneous societies to form one harmonious whole, which enjoys one common American culture—in order to hold a worthwhile discussion about the attitudes we've just delineated, we have to accept that "huddled masses" referenced almost exclusively those of Western European descent. Indeed, until 1952—little more than sixty years ago—every naturalization act passed by Congress included language that indicated any person who sought citizenship should be a "white person."

Over this sixty year period, there have been writers such as Howard Zinn, annual events such as Black History Month, and movements such as We Need Diverse Books that have attempted or are attempting to course correct, to strive toward the goal of including the broadest range of American voices in the collective narrative we tell ourselves. Even so, the fact remains that there is still a sort of default to the plot line of what has been the dominant culture for the last several hundred years.

To be sure, we've come a long way from the days when, though the United States was never an all-white nation, we played one on TV. When the American ideal was represented in the media by television shows like *Father Knows Best, Leave it to Beaver*, and *I Love Lucy*—shows that mirrored the ideals and aspirations of the white majority, if not necessarily the reality in which that majority actually lived. In those days when Blacks were cast in television and movie roles, it was almost exclusively as housemaids and butlers. Even shows with a majority Black cast, like Beulah, which was about the woman who was the maid and cook for the white Henderson family. Amos and Andy, another popular show of the time, so relentlessly portrayed Black men as shiftless and lazy that the U.S. Army asked ABC to stop running it because it assaulted the morale of Black soldiers. "For thirteen months, I was the Jackie Robinson of television," Nat King Cole, one of the legendary entertainers of the 20th century, said in a 1958 interview in *Ebony* magazine about his short-lived television show. "After a trail-blazing year that shattered all the old bug-a-boos about Negroes on TV, I found myself standing there

with the bat on my shoulder," was the way he described
hosting his own variety program on NBC, a program that
presented him as neither a caricature or stereotype but simply as a talented and popular performer in his own right—
and which was cancelled because the network couldn't find
a national sponsor willing to deal with the backlash from
viewers in the segregated South. So many rejected this or-
dinary, free-from-stereotype image of a Black man that
NBC was forced to take the image down.

Black entertainers are, these days, allowed more
three-dimensionality, and Black sports figures are certainly
mainstream. We have made great strides across many social and cultural areas since the movements of the 1960s,
but that is not so when it comes to our politics. Indeed,
when it comes to our politics, it can feel as if we are still
living in some lost TV land where challenging the dominance of the straight, white patriarchy can get you cancelled. Commentators on certain news shows still discuss
with straight faces the pros and cons of paying women
the same amount men are paid to do the same job; the fa-
bled American melting pot turns cold when the immigrant
isn't a white European but a brown Mexican; whether gay
people should enjoy civil rights is a matter up for debate
from religion to religion, and sometimes from denomination to denomination within the same religion. In our politics, we're still fighting not only the battles of the 1960s but
also those of the 1860s. Nationally, our politics are as segregated today as they were nearly three generations ago.

Now, you might say, but wait a minute, we have a Black
president. Doesn't that prove we're moving forward in our

politics? I would answer that, yes... maybe, it does. But I would also argue that the people who are opposed to progress, who are still invested in the dominant narrative, who retain a sense of proprietorship about their ownership of it, have found an acceptable and credible vehicle for their resistance to and resentment of the changing narrative in the person of our first Black president.

BEFORE WE GET into the heart of the book and our discussion of resistance and resentment, however, let's take a step back and talk a little bit about *why* the narrative is changing at all.

First, we have demographics.

The numbers are striking. In the U.S., by the year 2050, according to the U.S. Census Bureau, Blacks, Asians, Hispanics, Native Americans, and Pacific Islanders will, collectively, make up a larger percentage of the U.S. population than will whites. A shift in the demographics among children under eighteen years old will happen even sooner— the members of these formerly minority groups will outnumber whites by the year 2023. In the years between 2000 and 2007 the "minority" population in the U.S. grew at nearly three times the rate of the total population— from 28.6% of the population in 2000 to over 31%, where it stood in 2014. In Texas and California, the two largest states in the nation, the "minority" population already makes up the majority.

The inevitability of no longer being in the majority has some among that former majority so stressed out that

Fig. 2.   The U.S. is Experiencing Rapid Diversification

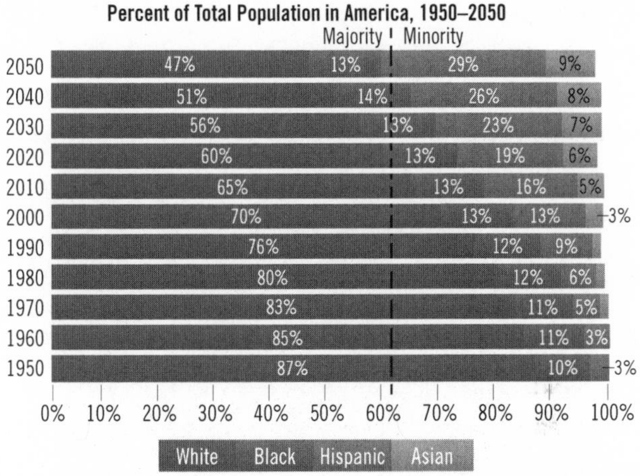

Percent of Total Population in America, 1950–2050

Year	Majority	Minority		
	White	Black	Hispanic	Asian
2050	47%	13%	29%	9%
2040	51%	14%	26%	8%
2030	56%	13%	23%	7%
2020	60%	13%	19%	6%
2010	65%	13%	16%	5%
2000	70%	13%	13%	3%
1990	76%	12%	9%	
1980	80%	12%	6%	
1970	83%	11%	5%	
1960	85%	11%	3%	
1950	87%	10%	3%	

there is even a catch-all term for their condition: white anxiety. White anxiety, as we've seen it demonstrated so far, hasn't taken the form of overt claims of white superiority. Rather, it is manifested through grievance (e.g., Sarah Palin's admonishment to the President to "stop playing the race card"[29]), victimhood (e.g., Ross Douthat's claim that institutions of higher learning are discriminating against whites in their admissions policies[30] and Donald Trump's assertion that a brown-skinned judge couldn't possibly give him a fair hearing about his fraud charges[31]), and blatant fear mongering (Rush Limbaugh's assertion that angry blacks are training their children to be future militants[32]). We hear white anxiety in every scream to "take the country back." From Republican politicians running on a platform of "take back the country,"[33] to right-wing media types holding forth at "Taking Our Country Back" rallies,[34] to country singers composing original ditties on the theme,[35] to rank-and-file "Tea Party Patriots" waving signs bearing the slogan, the sentiment has become ubiquitous in certain quarters. But what do "Tea Party Patriots" mean when they say it? When you get to the heart of it, what—or who—are they taking their country back *from?*

That's the second part of the answer to our question: they want to take their country back from former minorities who are in the process of finding their power in growing numbers, and exercising it in the voting booth.

At Tendly Baptist Church, in Philadelphia, Pennsylvania, on January 16, 1984, Jesse Jackson declared himself a candidate for president of the United States in a speech that has become famous in American rhetoric—and that first laid out the possibilities of what could happen to electoral politics if minorities, as well as young people, understood the power their combined numbers could wield at the ballot box. "In 1980," Jackson told the crowd, "Reagan won Massachusetts by 2,500 votes! There were over a hundred thousand students unregistered, over 50,000 blacks, over 50,000 Hispanics. He won by 2,500. Ted Kennedy's state. Rocks just laying around.

"He won Illinois by 300,000 votes—800,000 unregistered blacks, 500,000 Hispanics, rocks just laying around!

"In 1980 three million high school students unregistered to vote. Now they've registered to draft. Rocks still laying around! Eleven million college students who could have chosen jobs over jails, peace over war, that didn't vote. Now they're crying. Rocks just laying around!

"Reagan won eight southern states by 182,000 votes when there were three million unregistered blacks in those same eight states. Rocks just laying around!

"He won New York by 165,000 votes. 600,000 students unregistered, 900,000 blacks, 600,000 Hispanics. Rocks just laying around!

"In 1980, Reagan won Pennsylvania by 300,000 votes, 400,000 students unregistered. More than 600,000 blacks unregistered! Reagan won Pennsylvania by the margin of despair, by the margin of the fracture of our coalition."

The real strategic brilliance of the Obama campaign, when you cut through all the clutter, is that we did a better job of picking up those rocks than any other presidential campaign in history. The almost hysterical antagonism that attends President Obama's governance is based in already-existing attitudes about race that the powers behind the "Tea Party" have been able to masterfully exploit—and their task was made even less daunting, however, by shifting demographics in the U.S.: America's change, its *rapid* change, from a white majority nation. The coalition that Jackson envisioned fully crystalized in 2008, under the leadership of Barack Obama. A majority of the nation rejoiced at the election of America's first Black president. But, for another segment of the population, Barack Obama became the personification of the catastrophe that Jesse Jackson foretold. It was a calamity.

In order to appreciate the scope of the calamity these people are experiencing, we have to understand that they view this political turn as, truly, a *threat*—a threat to their way of life, to their comfort and privilege. Some people respond to the perceived threat with hateful words alone: "The days of [minorities] not having any power are over, and they are angry. And they want to use their power as a means of retribution. That's what Obama's about, gang. He's angry; he's going to cut this country down to size. He's going to make it pay for all the multicultural mistakes that it has made—its mistreatment of minorities. I know exactly what's going on here."[36] Other people—the three Staten Island men who beat up a teenager on Election Day for no other reason than that he was, like the new president-elect, Black, or the gunman who killed nine parishioners at Mother Emanuel—translate the hateful words into action.

But make no mistake about it, no matter the tools they employ to mitigate an event they experience as calamity—a handgun deployed in an historic Black church or laws deployed to restrict minority voting rights—the intent is the same: to limit the power and influence and even the sheer number of a group or groups of people they view as "other", different from themselves, and therefore unworthy of not only holding high office, but of having a voice in the election of those who do hold office.

2

The Southern Strategy

> **"We've lost the South for a generation."**

*Lyndon Johnson, remarks on signing
the 1964 Civil Rights Act*

> **"You start out in 1954 by saying, 'Nigger, nigger, nigger.' By 1968 you can't say "nigger"—that hurts you, backfires. So you say stuff like, uh, forced busing, states' rights, and all that stuff, and you're getting so abstract. Now, you're talking about cutting taxes, and all these things you're talking about are totally economic things and a byproduct of them is, blacks get hurt worse than whites.... 'We want to cut this,' is much more abstract than even the busing thing, uh, and a hell of a lot more abstract than 'Nigger, nigger.'"**

Lee Atwater, 1981, on "the Southern Strategy"

Long before the world had ever heard of a man named Barack Obama—indeed, before Barack Obama was even born—there was a scheme called the Southern Strategy that the Republican party put to good use in election cycle after election cycle, coolly and methodically co-opting the votes of racially resentful whites by using coded, or "dog whistle", language that evoked the most egregious of racial stereotypes, but always couching the underlying racism by framing their "concerns" as economic ones.

Before we dissect the Strategy, however, it will be helpful to understand the background from which it was created. The history is important because the racial tensions that plague our country—and, specifically, the Obama presidency—did not arise wholly from the superficial differences among races but is, rather, a political construct.

First of all, while the contemporary Republican Party, as a whole, is more Southern and more conservative, more aged and more white than ever before, it wasn't always the case that the party actively sought to disengage from Black or other minority voters. The Republican Party was founded, after all, in 1854, with ending slavery as one of its principal objectives—and in this goal, headed by Abraham Lincoln, it succeeded. After the Civil War, carpetbaggers—a general term coined to describe Yankees, often Republican political appointees, who moved to the South during Reconstruction—frequently relocated with the dual goals of profiting from the power vacuum that existed there after the Civil War and a genuine desire to help improve the lives of the newly freed slaves. They welcomed Black men into electoral politics for the first time, and the

members of the GOP in Washington led the fight to rat-
ify the 13th,[37] 14th,[38] and 15th[39] Amendments which abolished slavery, recognized Black men as full citizens, and
gave them the franchise. The loyalty of the Black population to the Party of Lincoln had been carved out—but not
set in stone.

A scant twenty-two years later, during the contested
presidential election of Rutherford B. Hayes, an Ohio Republican strongly supported by Northern industrialists,
came the Compromise of 1876. The Compromise called
for Hayes to recall all federal troops from the South in exchange for Southern Democrats withdrawing their opposition to his election—a compromise under which Southern
politicians, referred to as "redeemer Democrats", created
new state constitutions, passed new voter registration laws
to make voting more difficult for African-Americans, and
ushered in the age of "Jim Crow".

Jim Crow—named for a character invented by the min-
strel performer Thomas Dartmouth Rice (1808–1860)
whose "Jim Crow" was a broad racial caricature intended to
flatter the then-contemporary conceit of white superiority—was a series of laws, statues, and ordinances enacted
in the years between 1874 and 1975 that codified racial segregation in the South. In theory, these laws were put in
place to uphold the ruling of the Supreme Court—*Plessy
v. Ferguson* (1896)—which required "separate but equal" facilities for Blacks and whites. This meant that Blacks and
whites attended different schools, sat in different parts of
the theater, ate in different parts of the restaurant, stayed
at different hotels and/or entered them by way of different

doors, drank from different water fountains, swam in different community pools, and—famously—sat, or stood, in different parts of the bus.[40] In practice, of course, these laws created nothing like a "separate but equal" environment; Jim Crow fated Blacks to both inferior facilities, and inferior treatment.

In response to the Jim Crow laws enacted by the "redeemer Democrats", and in order to compete for the votes of Southern whites who benefitted from them, the Republican Party purged itself of its Black membership.

In the ensuing years—with the notable exception of the 1922 passage of the Dyer Anti-Lynching Bill—government paid scant attention to issues that impacted Black citizens, again with one notable but subtle exception. In an event known as the Great Migration, Blacks were leaving the South, moving to Northern and Midwestern urban areas as well as West, to California and other Western states. In the years between 1910 and 1930, 1.6 million Blacks left the rural South, and in the years between 1940 and 1970, another five million moved away from their Southern roots. When they got to their new homes, Northern Democratic bosses welcomed the newcomers, both their aspirations and their demands, into their machines while their Republican counterparts were indifferent, at best, to Black participation. Allegiance to a political party is customarily based upon sharing that party's philosophy, or platform— and upon how that platform impacts the manner in which the individual is able to live what he or she considers his best life. That is, people tend to vote their own interests, or whatever they perceive their interests to be. The Party of

Fig. 3.   White Voting Pattern

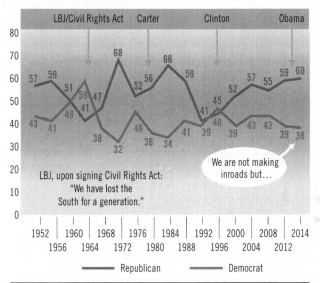

Lincoln was sorely testing the allegiance of its Black membership.

Then, in 1948, Harry Truman, a Democrat, desegregated the U.S. military, and the Democratic Party added a civil rights plank to its national platform. These actions created another catastrophic moment for Southern whites, then residents of what was known as the "Solid South" for the reliability of its Democratic voting pattern. Southern whites, feeling fully entitled to the perks of being white under Jim Crow, began to drift away from affiliation with the Democratic Party. In fact, this was the point at which the States' Rights Democratic Party, known colloquially as the "Dixiecrat" Party, was formed. Dixiecrats were a segregationist faction of the Democratic Party that sought to preserve a "Southern way of life" they believed under siege by racial integration—and a political party as well as a federal government that seemed more and more to support desegregation. The Dixiecrat party was short-lived—however the term remained in popular use through the 1990s to refer to more conservative Southern Democrats—but the racial resentment that it had fomented was not.

The Roots of the Southern Strategy

The 1964 Civil Rights Act was enacted on July 2nd of that year. Following the passage of that monumental legislation, fears rose afresh among many white Southerners who were still entrenched in, and still dependent upon, the tyrannical ways of Jim Crow. It was so clear that Southern whites would see this legislation as yet one more blow to their "way of life" that President Lyndon Johnson—himself a Southerner, and therefore tuned in to Southern thought—remarked that, by signing the law, he had "... lost the South for a generation" for Democratic politicians. As we now know, his estimate of the time it would take to heal the country's racial rift was decidedly optimistic. And as a matter of fact, what LBJ should have said was "there goes the white vote" as Democrats at the presidential level have not won white voters since that monumentally transformative legislative act.

As the Civil Rights Act went into effect, politicians on both sides of the aisle began to analyze its impact on their chances for success at the polls. Two dominant constituent groups were now up for competition: white Southerners who were bitter towards the Civil Rights Act, and African-Americans who had gained from the act the right to perform the civic duty of voting. A Democratic president had signed the bill—albeit, I hasten to add, a bill that had been passed with the help of key Republicans such as Senator Everett Dirkson of Illinois[41]—and, so, the Democratic Party enjoyed full credit for it. But the question now arose among Republicans: which constituent group—those who despised the bill or those who benefitted from it—should Republicans capitalize on for votes?

As Linwood Holton noted in a 2002 *New York Times* opinion piece, "An End to the Southern Strategy?," the question was: "Should Republicans take advantage of Southern Democrat resentment over the civil rights movement by luring white Southern racists into the fold? Or should it seek to build the party by doing just the opposite: opening its arms to African-American voters?" As Senator Dirksen himself might have pointed out, it was a choice between embracing an idea whose time had come, or being left on the wrong side of history; sadly—cynically—the Republican Party chose the latter. As Holton, the Republican governor of Virginia from 1970 through 1974, explains it, the GOP's "...tactic was simple: lace your speeches with coded appeals to racists in southern states, dressing the policies up in the language of fiscal conservatism." According to Joseph Aistrup, author of *The Southern Strategy Revisited*, "The major goal of the Southern Strategy was to transform the Republicans' reputation as the party of Lincoln, Yankees, and carpetbaggers into the party

that protects white interests." It banked on the boiling over
of race relations in the southern region, and "the liberaliz-
ing changes in the national Democrat's policy positions"[42]
to aid in the transformation.

The problem with this decision was evident: it would
exclude African-American support for the Republican Par
ty for years to come, and it would also appeal only to
that generation of extreme Southern white racists—and
only for as long as they were living. The Republican Party,
however, did not let go of this tactic after a generation, as
President Johnson had predicted so hopefully; it has tried
to hold on to this method since Richard Nixon's 1968 presidential campaign, refusing to adjust to the changing times
and direction—and demographics—of the country. In this
way, it has helped to prolong the era of racial tensions, even
helping to create ever newer generations of tribal political
warriors—happy to let the pot of racial tension simmer,
and stirring it up at election time, when they calculate it is
to their advantage to do so.

The modern Southern Strategy, however, did not make
its debut in the 1968 election. According to Aistrup, "Significantly, the GOP began a conscious effort to recast their
Southern image after Nixon's loss in 1960." Under the influence of Goldwater and his allies, the Republican National Committee's (RNC) program, "Operation Dixie"
openly promoted more conservative states' rights and segregationist policies, according to Aistrup, and recruited
candidates that were comfortable promoting these sort

of policies. Indeed, placing race as the central variable in their political strategy has been without question one of the most effective political practices in modern politics—up until 2008, when President Obama and his team saw all the "rocks just laying around" and picked them up.

The Southern Strategy did not become solid, however, until 1964. At this point the Republicans began promoting segregationist politics hidden behind economic terms, opposing such policy positions as forced busing, employment quotas, and affirmative action. While Nixon's 1968 presidential campaign is generally seen as the first political campaign to effectively use the Southern Strategy, it was Senator Barry Goldwater's 1964 presidential campaign that laid the groundwork for this particular tactic. The Senator from Arizona said, in 1961, when speaking to a group of Republican leaders in Atlanta, "We're not going to get the Negro vote as a bloc in 1964 and 1968, so we ought to go hunting where the ducks are."[43] The "ducks", in this case, were, in particular, racially averse Southerners; the beginning of the modern Southern Strategy can be tied to that very statement.

Goldwater lost tremendously to Lyndon Johnson, and carried only five states in the South, so it's reasonable to wonder why the takeaway from his campaign carried over for years to come—why it has now lasted for almost fifty years, and counting. I say "and counting" because right now Trump is expanding or updating the Southern Strategy—the Southern Strategy 2.0, if you will, to add both Hispanics and Muslims to the polarized us-versus-them tribal divide.

The Southern Strategy Solidifies

The Republican National Committee's "Operation Dixie" was the method the party settled on to implement the Southern Strategy. And as Aistrup pointed out, originally, back in 1957, "it was an attempt to build on Eisenhower's popularity in the South by creating a moderate-to-conservative, 'non-racist' Southern Republican party." Following Richard Nixon's loss in 1960, however, the RNC drafted a number of theories as to why they encountered this loss. Barry Goldwater's theory took the lead. He firmly believed that what the Republican Party needed was the Southern vote. He also felt that Nixon, or any other candidate who ran on their platform, could be more appealing to white voters if the platform shied away from support of civil rights. Not all elected officials within the party aligned with these new views, of course. Senator Sherman Cooper from Kentucky was quoted by Aistrup as stating "...such a position will destroy the Republican Party, and worse, it will do a great wrong because it will be supporting the denial of constitutional and human rights of our citizens." But voices such as Cooper's did not prevail within the party.

WHEN THE RHETORIC of his campaign was studied by several authors and journalists long after the fact, Goldwater's 1964 presidential campaign is said to have focused on leaving "audiences indistinguishable from their leader in many ways. They [audience members] were optimistic, active, bold, energetic, positive, willing to take an unpopular stand for a moral cause and in possession of simple truths." This cultivation of audience affinity was an approach another one of the major architects of the Southern Strategy during the Nixon era, Kevin Phillips, would take to heart— and brilliantly exploit.

Phillips, who had started off as an administrative assistant to Congressman Paul Fino of the Bronx, also grew up in the Bronx. It was there that he realized that most groups voted on the "basis of ethnic or cultural enmities that could be graphed, predicted and exploited."[44] Phillips encouraged his Congressman to remove himself from his "liberal" standpoints and instead oppose programs that President Johnson's Great Society opened up, mainly school funding and the war on poverty. Phillips had concluded that not only was opposition to Great Society programs increasing even among residents of the northeast (although mainly those of European descent), but that this opposition formed blocks of turnout majorities among voters in favor of candidates who publicly denounced such programs. Phillips wanted to play on the changing tide among the area's demographics. Irish, Italian, and other European immigrants who had for generations voted along the then-current Democratic Party lines in the New York area were beginning to resent the group that primarily benefited from the Civil Rights Act and the reforms of the Great Society. Phillips used this growing resentment and frustration to pivot votes and direct a new following towards the Republican Party.

Serving as a strategist for Richard Nixon's 1968 presidential campaign, Phillips was quoted as giving this advice to the Presidential candidate: "From now on, the Republicans are never going to get more than 10 to 20 percent of the Negro vote and they don't need any more than that... but Republicans would be shortsighted if they weakened enforcement of the Voting Rights Act. The more Negroes who register as Democrats in the South, the sooner the Negrophobe whites will quit the Democrats and become Republicans. That's where the votes are. Without that prodding from the blacks, the whites will backslide into their old comfortable arrangement with the local Democrats."[45]

In Phillips's opinion, there were layers to the Southern Strategy, starting with what was termed the Outer South Strategy. The Outer South Strategy targeted white groups in some outlying states such as Florida, Tennessee, North Carolina, Appalachia, and Virginia. Phillips felt it was important to start campaign mobilization around groups that were less extreme and then proceed to draw in the most conservative of groups. He felt he had a good foothold as "the general conservative economic disposition of the New South was more in tune with the Republican party."[46] Focusing first on notions that appealed to urban Southerners would provide the GOP with a real foot in the door—an opening to the new demographic following and numbers that they would need to gain power.

As a strategist, he could not have had his finger more accurately on the zeitgeist.

The election of Richard Nixon in 1968 happened in the midst of turmoil—and it created turmoil in its own right. The election took place against a background of violence—the assassinations of the Democratic candidate for the presidency, Robert F. Kennedy, and Martin Luther King, the unrest that followed the assassination of the civil rights leader, university campuses that were erupting in widespread opposition to the war in Vietnam, and vicious confrontations between anti-war protestors and the police at the Chicago 1968 Democratic Convention.

This was also the election where an incumbent president—and one who had won by a landslide only four years earlier—was forced out of the race.

Richard Nixon didn't abandon the Southern Strategy after he was elected, either. Once in office, he employed it as a governing tactic, the first presidency in which the Southern Strategy was officially used in office. Having run against Alabama Governor George Wallace in the Republican primary during the 1968 election, Nixon now adopted Wallace's pivot for denying Blacks civil rights, aligning "the perceived social costs thrust on the common white man for achieving racial equity goals."[47] For example, while in office, Nixon publicly denounced court-ordered school busing on national TV, referring to it as a symbol of "helplessness" and using phrases such as "wrenching of children away from their families" to gain support in opposition to court-ordered busing and thus appealing to the heart of middle America, who may have been seeing these changes take place in their own communities.[48] Instead of blatantly attacking minority groups and the gains made during the Johnson Presidency, Nixon sought to attack civil rights through the courts.

RONALD REAGAN, THE next Republican to campaign for and win the presidency after Nixon, also benefited from implementing the Southern Strategy, but his version of the tactic appealed to a larger audience than ever before. His administration realized "that a more direct assault on the policies of affirmative action would appeal to both Southern and Northern working-class whites."[49] Recognized for his great speaking skills, Reagan used rhetoric effectively to portray "the nature of governmental social services and the people served by them."[50] Given that stereotypes of those who receive governmental social services circulate around minority groups, Reagan was strategic in painting a picture of groups that were deserving and hardworking and those that were not. The ambiguity in the terms he used regularly such as "undeserving" or "greedy" is exactly what was most effective about his speech and its implications on Americans' way of thinking about the current state of the country. What is key in understanding the workings of the Reagan administration is that their policies were designed to have white Southern Democrats recognize that that their interests were also expressed within the Republican Party's framework. Playing on a values system within this particular demographic that included prayer in school and opposition to abortion and busing, states' rights were emphasized in what was termed the "New Right" coalition.[51] The numbers testify to how effective Reagan's rhetoric as president was to luring people into the Republican Party: between 1980 and 1996, 480,000 individuals became registered Republicans in comparison to only 33,000 people becoming registered Democrats.

RIDING ON THE coattails of Reagan's critical two terms, George H. W. Bush came into office using the same methods those before him had found so successful. His speaking skills in comparison to Reagan's might have been "callous and unrefined",[52] but he got his points across to the right audience—most infamously in the 1988 "Willie Horton" campaign ads.[53] These ads featured William R. "Willie" Horton, an African-American who was serving a life sentence for murder in the state of Massachusetts—the state in which Bush's opponent, Michael Dukakis, was governor, and on whose watch Horton was released under the state's furlough program. To be clear, Dukakis did not start this furlough program; Horton was released from prison under a program that had been signed into law under Republican governor Francis W. Sargent in 1972. But Horton did not return to prison when his weekend furlough ended; he remained at large for nearly a year, and committed various violent crimes in that time frame—including pistol-whipping, knifing, and rape—and ended up as the menacing Black face pinned to the charge that Dukakis was soft on crime. The message: if you didn't vote for Bush, a big intimidating Black man might come after you.

Bush was elected with 53.4% of the popular vote, and a whopping 426 votes in the Electoral College.

In 1990, he vetoed the extension of the Civil Rights Act, saying that it represented a quota bill—a bill that ultimately barred workplace discrimination against people who were disabled.

DURING THIS SAME time period, David Duke, a former Klansmen, and Republican Representative from Louisiana, emerged as a loud, racially radical voice within the GOP network. As Duke's notorious reputation grew publicly, the Bush administration began to distance itself from the congressman, noting that a "racially reactionary" elected official was damaging to the GOP. "'I could not possibly support David Duke,' Bush said, 'because of the racism and because of the very recent statements that are very troubling in terms of bigotry and all of this.'"[54] The irony in this is Duke's usage of the same terms that were so often uttered by President Bush himself. Bush themes, such as opposition to quotas and affirmative action, blaming government for the economy, and attacks of those on welfare, were all mirrored by David Duke when speaking to his Louisiana constituency. In other words, David Duke was saying exactly what the rest of the Republican Party was saying, only without the filter. This made the establishment uncomfortable—in the same way that, in 2016, the notoriously filter-less Donald Trump has caused the establishment members of his party to squirm as he expresses in plain words those sentiments they have kept coded for all these decades.

DURING PRESIDENT BUSH'S second campaign, in 1992, three critical talking points of the Southern Strategy were removed—"anticommunism, race, and taxes."[55] Clearly, this did not provide the party with enough momentum to reclaim the White House it had held for the last three terms.

Bill Clinton won that race, of course, with only 43% of the popular vote, and 370 electoral votes to George H. W. Bush's 168. To be clear, however, and despite what some others argue, I don't see how those white working-class males who bolstered Ross Perot's astonishing showing that year would have broken for Bill Clinton; they hadn't been breaking for Democrats and continue not to do so. Despite the political gifts and brilliance of Bill Clinton, Ross Perot helped take the White House away from H.W. Bush and the Bush campaign folks knew it. Since the rise of the Southern Strategy at the national level it has been foiled only by outlying phenomenon—the impeachment of Nixon and Ross Perot's garnering about nineteen million votes from the white electorate.[56]

In the second half of President Clinton's first term, however, Republicans took over the House of Representatives, with Newt Gingrich serving as Speaker of the House. In what was termed the "Contract with America", House GOP members continued to channel the sentiments of the Southern Strategy. The "Contract" focused on welfare reform, middle-class and capital gains tax cuts, crime prevention, and an increase in military spending, all of which was strongly supported by Republicans from the South—the result was that in the 1994 mid-term election, 65% of all white males voted for Republican members of Congress. The Southern Strategy effectively resurfaced once again.

The Death of the Southern Strategy

The Southern Strategy may continue to linger because many refuse to come to grips with not only its modern-day ineffectiveness, but its real and growing efficiency in losing elections for those who employ it. The most recent example of its usage is in the 2012 presidential campaign, during which President Obama, the target of the strategy, won handily—303 Electoral College votes to his opponent's 206, and the popular vote by over two percentage points.

Newt Gingrich, a candidate for the top Republican slot in 2012, referred to President Obama in a 2012 Republican Primary Debate in South Carolina as "the best food stamp president in American history"[57]—which was clearly a racial reference to both the president and some of his strongest supporters. The continuing rumor that Obama is a secret Muslim is an extremely strong evocation of the Southern Strategy, invoking nationalism and fear in a piece of propaganda that can easily be tied to an overseas enemy. The Romney/Ryan presidential campaign was, by far, of course, the biggest loser to try to use the Southern Strategy. From the infamous *Mother Jones* video in which Romney depicts 47% of Americans as being dependent and entitled to government handouts, to referring to Obama as gutting welfare-to-work requirements, to championing the elimination of Obamacare, a piece of legislation that positively impacts millions of minorities, Romney and company attempted to roil up feelings of frustration, ostensibly tied to the economy but which had underlying racial tones.[58]

What Romney and company didn't count on was voter

turnout—those damn "rocks just laying around" again that Jesse Jackson talked about, the very specific sort of turnout that their subtly Southern Strategy campaign tactics actually helped to increase. Indeed, on multiple occasions my Republican colleagues would come up to me with the claim that we/the Obama campaign couldn't and wouldn't reproduce the kinds of record turnout again in 2012 that we were able to produce in 2008. They were right, we couldn't; we *beat* our 2008 turnout. Fittingly, for the first time ever, Black voters outvoted whites in the 2012 presidential election. In 2012 the most likely voter was an African-American. #boom.

The impressive Black voter turnout in 2012 is not, however, without backlash. The contemporary voter-suppression efforts, targeting African-American voters and led by Republican governors and other legislators in states all across the country, are a direct response to white fear of losing political power in an era of riveting social and demographic change.

IN THE ERA of George W. Bush, an attempt was made to redeem the Republican Party. Ken Mehlman, the chairman of the Republican National Committee from 2005 to 2007, publicly apologized for the Southern Strategy during a speech at the NAACP's National Convention in 2005: "By the '70s and into the '80s and '90s, the Democratic Party solidified its gains in the African-American community, and we Republicans did not effectively reach out... Some Republicans gave up on winning the African-American vote, looking the other way or trying to benefit politically from racial polarization. I am here today as the Republican chairman to tell you we were wrong."[59]

This is noted as the first public denunciation of the Southern Strategy from the head of the Republican Party. In light of the social and demographic changes we're talking about in this book—and the current depth of the entrenchment of the Republican Party in racial antago-nism—it should probably not be the last if the GOP wants any hope of remaining a legitimate force in American pol-itics. Did anyone show Trump the much-publicized "Re-publican autopsy report" following the 2012 presidential election?

The Othering of Barack Obama

> **"**In all his imaginings, he had never envisioned her crying. He knew that her son had died, but he'd never expected that her pain might be anything he could recognize, almost as though he believed that Negroes had their own special kind of grieving ritual, another language, something other than tears they used to express their sadness.**"**

Bebe Moore Campbell, Your Blues Ain't Like Mine

> **"**But race is the child of racism, not the father.**"**

Ta-Nehisi Coates, Between the World and Me

What is "Race"?

The simple—and simply factual—answer to that question is: A myth.

If a guy from Norway and a woman from Zimbabwe have an "interaction"—as Bill Nye, the Science Guy, once so delicately put it on "The Nightly Show with Larry Wilmore"—what you're going to get, nine months later, is a human being. Thus, the renowned scientist debunked the entire idea of race: albeit some of us have different facial features or different skin tones, we humans are all one *species*, a word defined, in terms of its scientific usage, in the Merriam-Webster dictionary as "a group of animals or plants that are similar and can produce young animals and plants."

But those of us who make up the human species, *Homo sapiens*, are not always—or, at least, not always *quickly*— swayed by scientific fact. Think, for a moment, of the current debate about climate change: a stunning 97%[60] of scientists are in consensus that climate change is real, and that it is man-made, and that it presents problems and challenges that are tangible, severe, and immediate to those of us who would like our children and our grandchildren to be able to continue to live on the planet Earth. Yet, in 2014, a study by the Pew Research Center found that a mere 10% of Republicans believe that global warming is real[61]—and this willful denial of settled science has become orthodoxy for conservative pundits[62] as well as GOP candidates playing to their disbelieving base.[63]

This book, of course, isn't the place to debate the reason for this particular Republican orthodoxy. We can, however, speculate that, along with issues such as adjusting corporate tax schedules to appropriate levels or raising the minimum wage, the wellspring of climate denial is more related to the GOP "free market" orthodoxy than it is to directly obstructing President Obama's climate change initiatives—even while we also note that climate change denial by U.S. politicians is unique in the world ("Indeed, it is difficult to identify another major political party in any democracy as thoroughly dismissive of climate science as is the GOP here."[64]) and has certainly had a negative impact on Obama's ability to negotiate necessary climate change treaties ("One needn't spend much time in the main offices of one of the world's top weeklies to understand the real significance of this state of affairs. It poses an enormous problem to the leaders of the world's other major powers, and there is almost nothing they can do about it. ... Imagine the world's major powers sitting down in the early-20th century to negotiate a treaty on the law of the sea, only to have one of America's major political parties vow to defeat any settlement, on the grounds that the world is in fact flat."[65]). We can also note that as the GOP's Southern Strategy, with its intent to alienate Black voters, was not a good decision for the long game, climate denial is likely not a good long-term strategy either: Hart Research Associates conducted a poll in 2013 on behalf of the League of Conservation Voters and found that advertisements that link a candidate with climate change denial erode the credibility of that candidate *even among Republican voters.*[66]

Similarly, though the idea of race and racial stereotypes—and, thus, racism—persist even to this day, the science behind the question of whether there is such a thing as "race" was settled by an international panel of scientists—sociologists, psychologists, anthropologists, and geneticists—in 1950. Their statement, released by the United Nations Educational, Scientific and Cultural Organization

(UNESCO) on July 18, 1950, begins, "Scientists have reached general agreements in recognizing that mankind is one: that all men belong to the same species, *Homo sapiens*. It is further generally agreed among scientists that all men are probably derived from the same common stock; and that such differences as exist between different groups of mankind are due to the operation of evolutionary factors of differentiation such as isolation, the drift and random fixation of the material particles which control heredity (the genes), changes in the structure of these particles, hybridization, and natural selection. In these ways groups have arisen of varying stability and degree of differentiation which have been classified in different ways for different purposes."[67]

Before we talk about the "purposes" for which differentiations have led to classifications, let's have a quick discussion about what those differentiations are, and the evolutionary reasons for them.

The differentiations we're talking about are things such as facial features and skin tones—those outward, physical differences we have come to define collectively as "race"—for which there is an elegantly simple scientific explanation: they are a function of human adaptation, over time, to climate, diet, way of life, and migration. Skin color, for example, is the result of Vitamin D synthesis in the human body—humans whose ancestors lived in locales where there is lots of sunshine, and therefore high-level ultra-violet (UV) radiation, tend to have darker tones because the body does not need to absorb as much Vitamin D from the sun as it does in locales where sunshine is more rare. This is similar to the reason that the irises of people whose ancestors are from the extremes of northern Europe, where daylight is dim, are lighter than those from countries where daylight is more plentiful. The epicanthal fold—the fold of skin at the inner corner of the eye that is an Asian feature—was probably a useful adaptation given the windy conditions of northern Asia. For millennia, people who lived in northern Asia were isolated from people who lived in the extremes of northern Europe who were isolated from those who lived in tropical areas to the south; and, in isolation and over generations, the body's physical adaptations became inheritable in the same way that freckles, dimples, hairline shape, earlobe attachment, and left-handedness are passed on to children through the genes of their parents and grandparents.

So, why then *do* we classify human beings based on physical characteristics?

In order to understand the *purpose* of such classification, we'll turn to the American Anthropological Association. In this group's statement of May 17, 1998,[68] the scientists were quite direct in their assessment of why, although there are no overarching behaviors that correlate with so-called "racial" characteristics such as skin tone or eye shape, negative stereotypes involving such things as the intelligence, work ethic, sexual behaviors, aggression, economic ability, family cohesion, brain size, and law-abidingness continue to persist.

"Historical research," the AAA statement reads, "has shown that the idea of 'race' has always carried more meanings than mere physical differences; indeed, physical variations in the human species have no meaning except the social ones that humans put on them. Today scholars in many fields argue that 'race' as it is understood in the United States of America was a social mechanism invented during the 18th century to refer to those populations brought together in colonial America: the English and other European settlers, the conquered Indian peoples, and those peoples of Africa brought in to provide slave labor.

"From its inception, this modern concept of 'race' was modeled after an ancient theorem of the Great Chain of Being, which posited natural categories on a hierarchy established by God or nature. Thus 'race' was a mode of classification linked specifically to peoples in the colonial situation. It subsumed a growing ideology of inequality devised to rationalize European attitudes and treatment of the conquered and enslaved peoples. Proponents of slavery in particular during the 19th century used 'race' to justify the retention of slavery. The ideology magnified the differences among Europeans, Africans, and Indians, established a rigid hierarchy of socially exclusive categories, underscored and bolstered unequal rank and status differences, and provided the rationalization that the inequality was natural or God-given. The different physical traits of African-Americans and Indians became markers or symbols of their status differences.

"As they were constructing US society, leaders among European-Americans *fabricated* [my italics] the cultural/behavioral characteristics associated with each 'race,' linking superior traits with Europeans and negative and inferior ones to blacks and Indians. Numerous arbitrary and fictitious beliefs about the different peoples were institutionalized and deeply embedded in American thought."

And that, readers, is the history of American racism in just a few succinct and stunning paragraphs: our modern-day understanding of "race" is a social construct designed by our forefathers and foremothers in order to perpetuate a system of "racial" control. It's a system through which physical characteristics that evolved from the geographic isolation of our most ancient forebears continues to isolate us by those same biologically meaningless physical traits.

And it's a system that continues to serve those who descend from European immigrants to American shores—because, though our scientists gave us the evidence almost seventy years ago, the myth of "race" continues to be reinforced in American society, albeit often, these days, in ways more subtle than our colonial forebears employed.

Tribes

> **"**A tribe is a group of people connected to one another, connected to a leader, and connected to an idea. For millions of years, human beings have been part of one tribe or another. A group needs only two things to be a tribe: a shared interest and a way to communicate. **"**
>
> *Seth Godin*, Tribes, We Need You to Lead Us

Understanding that those characteristics we use to perceive "race" are meaningless, however, doesn't mean they don't matter. They do. And for two very distinct and different reasons: we humans desire community with those who share our interests and tastes, and we desire community with those who share our ethnic backgrounds.

Let's talk first about the community we crave with those who share our interests and tastes. Simply, we identify with, and find comfort in the company of others who are like us. In the vast majority of situations, our preference for others who are like us is benign, and even desirable. You and I cheer for the same college football team. We live in the same city. We work in the same field. We both enjoy hiking, or tasting microbrews, or the music of Bruce Springsteen. We have these things in common and, therefore, we appreciate each other's company on the hiking trail, or at a brewery, or during a concert. If you're a USC fan, you're probably going to have more fun if you go to the game with another Trojan fan rather than someone who routinely roots for Notre Dame. If you go to a Springsteen concert knowing you're going to leave hoarse from chanting for "Brooooce" all night long, you're unlikely to ask someone who likes only classical music to be your date. And, while to those of us who are Springsteen fans, the idea of someone who doesn't like his music is truly baffling, it is also unlikely to make us actually *hate* the person who'd rather go hear an evening of Brahms.

Most of us have many such tribes—a group with whom you go to basketball games because you all like basketball, a group with whom you go to adventurous new restaurants because you all like trying new and adventurous foods, a group with whom you can talk about a shared interest in particular books or vintage cars or your similar career paths and so forth; it's unlikely that there is one single person on the face of the Earth who shares every single one of our individual interests, or needs, with us.

Among our tribes is often one that consists of people who share our ethnic backgrounds. There are foods, music, ways of worship, whole cultural and social histories we share with these people that evoke pride, comfort, and our understanding of the world at its deepest level—and enjoying communion with them is by no means a negative state of affairs.

For the first few hundred years of America's life, the country thought of itself as a "melting pot"—a place where very diverse groups came together to form one homogeneous society. It was a good metaphor for a concept that wasn't, at its heart, ignoble, but at the end of the day what it entailed was that immigrants were expected to, within a few generations at least, give up the cultural identities that made them unique and assimilate by adopting American lifestyles. In practice, and infamously, each new group of immigrants to the American shores was met with some level of hostility upon its arrival. National quotas were established in the early-20th century that promoted immigration from Britain, Ireland, and Germany, and discouraged Poles, Italians, and Russians; however, because whiteness was considered the norm in American society, each of these groups eventually managed some level of acculturation. In the 1880s, laws were enacted to restrict immigration from China, and the proliferation, as well as endurance, of "Chinatowns" as ethnic enclaves in America's larger cities stand as evidence that the hostility they faced was greater than that of European and Eastern European immigrants. Native Americans, though of course not immigrants, and Blacks faced even more daunting hurdles.

Due to the ease of global travel and the expansion of global trade, not to mention the ease with which technology now allows us to communicate with each other, America is slowly moving past the "melting pot" metaphor—itself a form of ethnocentrism in which we judge another culture based solely on the language and values and standards of the prevailing majority culture—and toward ones that signal a new appreciation for cultural distinctness as encapsulated in the concept of multiculturalism—for example, "cultural mosaic" and "salad bowl". Multiculturalism promotes the acceptance and respect for multiple cultural traditions within a shared geography. It encourages the exploration of and appreciation for dissimilar cultures. It, famously, "celebrates diversity"! Because we are no longer living on a planet in which groups of people are culturally isolated from one another, and because this planet would be a sadder and less beautiful place if we didn't preserve the stunning mosaic of really exceptional traditions that each culture offers, moving away from an ideal of assimilation toward one in which diversity is celebrated is a hugely positive development.

What isn't positive is that those meaningless physical traits by which one ethnic group differs from another are often still used to define the group, not only culturally but temperamentally, intellectually, and emotionally. And

those traits become the basis for "othering" a whole segment of the American population.

> **"**Unlike many White naitonalists [sic] I am of the
> opinion that the majority of American and European
> jews are White. In my opinion the issues with jews
> is not their blood, but their identity. I think that if we
> could somehow destroy the jewish identity, then they
> wouldnt cause much of a problem. The problem is that
> Jews look White, and in many cases are White, yet
> they see themselves as minorities. Just like niggers,
> most jews are always thinking about the fact that they
> are jewish. The other issue is that they network. If
> we could somehow turn every jew blue for 24 hours,
> I think there would be a mass awakening, because
> people would be able to see plainly what is going on. **"**

—from the manifesto of Dylan Roof

All Native Americans are gamblers and drunks. All
Middle Eastern people hate Americans and are terrorists.
All Hispanics are illegal aliens, and all male Hispanic immigrants are rapists. All women are highly emotional. All
Blacks are lazy and like living on welfare. All people who
speak with a Southern accent are slow-witted, ignorant
rednecks.

Xenophobia is the unreasonable fear or hatred of that
which is unfamiliar to us, that which differs from the society that prevails around us, and is, therefore, "other" than

we are. The easier it is to physically distinguish a group of people from ourselves, the easier it is to "other" them. And "othering" is, simply, an excellent and effective way to keep one group of people separate and suspicious of another group. That's because, when we "other", we assume the superiority of the group in which we ourselves belong. Tim Hunt, a male scientist, believes that male scientists are superior to female scientists.[69] Donald Trump, a white, believes that Blacks and Hispanics are more violent than whites—and asserts that these two groups of people account for 98% of violent crime.[70] Bill O'Reilly, a Catholic, believes that Islam "allows terror murder."[71]

We "other" people when we assign characteristics and behaviors not to individuals but to whole classes of people, and then, importantly, *judge* them as a group based upon those characteristics and behaviors. These characteristics and behaviors are, much more often than not, negative or inferior to those we would want assigned to "us."

Historically whites have held a host of negative stereotypes of Blacks, focusing on the perceived inferiority of Blacks with regard to multiple characteristics. For example, Blacks have traditionally been seen as less intelligent than whites, less industrious, and more violent. While white attitudes towards Blacks have improved over time, there is solid evidence that these stereotypes persist to this day.

The General Social Survey (GSS) is an academic standard that has consistently measured stereotypes of various groups over time. With regard to whites' perceptions of Blacks, the GSS shows that whites believe African-Americans are significantly less intelligent than they themselves are. When rating the perceived intelligence of both whites and Blacks, whites have consistently, since measurement began in 1990, rated Blacks lower. On the GSS seven-point scale in 2006, ranging from unintelligent to intelligent, whites rated Blacks as a 4.2. Whites rated their own group, on the other hand, a 4.58—a significant difference.

Blacks fare no better in whites' eyes on their willingness to work hard, helping to further fuel negative attitudes. Here again, according to GSS data, since 1990 whites have consistently rated themselves as more hardworking than they rate Blacks. In fact, in every measure since then whites have rated Blacks as significantly lower than the mid-point on the GSS lazy-to-hardworking scale. In 2006 whites rated Blacks a 2.74 while rating themselves a 3.48, another highly significant discrepancy.

Closely related to the belief that Blacks are not as hardworking as whites is the idea that African-Americans may be disadvantaged in our society, but if they are it is primarily because of their own lack of effort. When a CBS News poll asked as recently as January 2012 whether whites or Blacks have a better chance of getting ahead in American society, 38% of whites felt that their group fares better than Blacks, while another 52% said the chances were equal for each group. Only 9% of whites believed that Blacks had the better chance. If anyone is to blame for this situation, however, white public opinion says it is Blacks themselves: according to the Pew Research Center for the People and the Press, in January 2012, 63% of white Americans believed that Blacks not trying hard enough was more to blame for their not getting ahead than any racial discrimination.

Intelligence and industry are two traits that nearly every human being who's ever lived would like ascribed to him/herself. If we ourselves are among that group that values intelligence and industry, then, whether we admit it or not, we look down upon persons we consider stupid or lazy—and we aren't eager to claim them as our peers. They don't fit in with us; they are different from us, less than us. "Other" than us.

"Othering" strips dignity, and often simple humanity, from the excluded person. When we apply the concept to an entire group of people in one fell swoop, we negate the need to consider the dignity, and humanity, of every member of that group.

"OTHERING" POLITICAL CANDIDATES is nothing really new. In fact, you could say there's a fine tradition about it. For instance, though John F. Kennedy is now commonly considered one of our nation's greatest presidents, during his race for the White House he was "othered" for his Catholicism.

The practice of "othering" Catholics has its roots in the Reformation, and immigrants from Britain and Germany brought the practice with them to the New World. The budding majority Protestant nation had theological differences with Catholicism, of course, but they also had political concerns—that Catholics would always be more loyal to the influence of the Vatican, or Pope, than to the leaders of, or the constitution of, the United States. Let's remember that Martin Luther published his Ninety-Five Theses in 1517 as we move through time to 1960, when JFK's presidency began to realize how deep those roots were: in September of 1959, a group of 150 Protestant ministers met in Washington, D.C. and "declared that Kennedy could not remain independent of Church control unless he specifically repudiated its teachings."[72] Lest you think that the election of JFK put the issue to rest, James Martin, SJ, offered this analysis for the continuing "otherness" of Catholics in America forty years later: "...the Catholic Church is still seen as profoundly 'other' in modern culture and is therefore an object of continuing fascination. As already noted, it is ancient in a culture that celebrates the new, professes truths in a postmodern culture that looks skeptically on any claim to truth and speaks of mystery in a rational, post Enlightenment world."[73]

THE "OTHERING" OF Barack Obama did not begin immediately as he announced his candidacy. There was a novelty to the question, "Can a Black person be president of the United States?" And the novelty had a different texture to it than any other time in history when the question had been asked. From the time that Frederick Douglass garnered his one lone vote at the 1888 Republican convention to when Shirley Chisholm tossed her hat into the ring in 1972, there was, simply, very little chance that that particular question could be answered in the affirmative. Even when Jesse Jackson ran in 1984 and 1988, garnering in those primaries, respectively, three million and seven million votes, the possibility that he would make it through a general election was slim—at the time less than 77% of American voters said they would be willing to vote for a Black candidate. By 2008, however, that number had increased to 93% and, for the first time, the novelty of the question was asked within a reality where, theoretically, at least, electing a Black president was possible—at least to the portion of the population whose imaginations were ignited by such a possibility.

Article Two of the United States Constitution sets forth the eligibility requirements for a person to seek the office of president of the United States: "No person except a natural born Citizen, or a Citizen of the United States, at the time of the Adoption of this Constitution, shall be eligible to the Office of President; neither shall any Person be eligible to that Office who shall not have attained to the Age of thirty-five Years, and been fourteen Years a Resident within the United States." While birth records, school records, and employment records existed for Barack Obama, as they do for every other United States citizen who was born in the last hundred years or so, Obama was Black, and therefore an easier target to "other" than any serious presidential candidate had been before him. Additionally, he had a father who was a citizen of another country—the Harvard-educated, senior Kenyan government economist, Barack Obama, Sr. For those looking to throw shade on the idea that Barack Obama, Jr. had been "natural born", this was all they needed.

This "othering," in the sense that I am using the term here, is deliberately creating the idea of an alien other to reinforce difference and promote social and political dominance over the one deemed other or alien.[74]

Dr. Susan Brooks Thistletwaite, The
Islamic Monthly, June 15, 2012

Though Barack Hussein Obama never made an issue of hiding his middle name, Chris Matthews, an MSNBC news anchor (and no conservative) is often credited with the first public citation of it, on September 7, 2006: "You know, it's interesting that Barack Obama's middle name is Hussein. That'll be interesting down the road, won't it?"[75]

On September 24, 2006, Jennifer Senior referenced the middle name issue again in her article for *New York* magazine, "Dreaming of Obama": "So much hope and so much fuss. All over a man whose father was from Kenya and whose mother might have been a distant relation of Jefferson Davis. Whose meals in Indonesia were served, for a time, by a male servant who sometimes liked to wear a dress. Whose first and last names inconveniently rhyme with "Iraq Osama." And whose middle name, taken from his Muslim grandfather, is, of all things, Hussein. Where else but here, though, right?"

Maureen Dowd, in her *New York Times* opinion piece, December 2, 2006, got right to the point, opening her column with the declaration: "If you call Barack Obama's office to check the spelling of his middle name, the reply comes back: 'Like the dictator.'

"In the first rush of our blind date with the young senator from Illinois, we are still discovering things that are going to take some getting used to. Like his middle name: Hussein.

"There were already a few top Democrats scoffing at the idea that a man whose surname sounded like a Middle East terrorist could get elected president. Now it turns out that his middle name sounds like a Middle East dictator. So with one moniker, he evokes both maniacal villains of the Bush administration."

Dowd went on to note that "Republican wizards have whipped up nasty soufflés with far less tasty ingredients than that," though her column was written in response to a goodie that was already baking in the oven. Earlier in that week, Ed Rogers, an official in George Herbert Walker Bush's administration, had identified himself as someone who had already counted "Barack Hussein Obama" out in the 2008 presidential race.[76] In spite of the truth that Obama had, at that point, held public office for nearly nine years—and had published his first book, a memoir, *Dreams from My Father*, over ten years earlier—Rogers insisted Obama was a "blank canvas" on which others could "project their desires." He was an "ideal candidate because nobody knows anything about him." And what Rogers wanted to make sure he projected onto the potential 2008 candidate, just in case anyone hadn't yet heard, was his middle name: Hussein.

"Hussein" is an Arabic name that is the diminutive of Hassan. It means "good." Its first recorded use was by the prophet Muhammad who named his grandson Husayn ibn Ali, as he was, according to lore, commanded to do by the archangel Gabriel. For Obama, it is a family name—he was named after his father, and it was his father's middle name.

But Barack Hussein Obama, Sr. was also a Muslim, as was the president's stepfather—and the president's stepfather was also Indonesian. Indonesia, a country with a majority Muslim population, is where the future president would, because of his mother's second marriage, spend a portion of his childhood. If Republicans were making a soufflé out of the fact that the candidate's middle name was Hussein, they were about to bake a thirteen-layer royal wedding cake with their attempts to take these sparse facts and, with them, turn Obama into a Muslim, a segment of the American population that had been not only efficiently "othered" but shamelessly vilified since 9/11.

The pile-on was immediate: "So, even if he identifies strongly as a Christian, and even if he despised the behavior of his father (as Obama said on Oprah); is a man who Muslims think is a Muslim, who feels some sort of psychological need to prove himself to his absent Muslim father, and who is now moving in the direction of his father's heritage, a man we want as President when we are fighting the war of our lives against Islam? Where will his loyalties be?

"Is that even the man we'd want to be a heartbeat away from the Presidency, if Hillary Clinton offers him the Vice Presidential candidacy on her ticket (which he certainly wouldn't turn down)?

"NO WAY, JOSE . . . Or, is that, HUSSEIN?"[77] asked Debbie Schlussel, a right-wing blogger in her post of December 18, 2006 that was titled "Once a Muslim Always a Muslim."

The opportunity to once again repeat Obama's middle name was one right-wing pundits just couldn't turn down, no matter how old that news was. Ann Coulter opined that Hillary Clinton was probably the real front-runner in the race based on "the fact that her leading Democratic opponent is named 'Barack Hussein Obama.'"[78] Rush Limbaugh suggested the candidate should be called "Barack Hussein Odumbo."[79] The host of Fox News's *Hannity & Colmes*, Sean Hannity, inquired disingenuously, "Now, if his middle name is Hussein, what is wrong with people that bring up his middle name?"[80]

These are merely the broad strokes of the way that the role of race impacted upon the coverage of the run-up to the 2008 presidential race, and then upon the race itself. There is one other incident, however, that demonstrates just how run-away the right-wing train was as its partisans attempted to disqualify the Black candidate from the field: the rumor that Obama had attended a madrassa.

Madrassa is the Arabic word that refers to any sort of educational institution, whether religious or secular, but in the context of the American nightly news circa 2007, madrassa had a more specific if untrue definition: a school in which radical fundamentalist Islam is the emphasized course of study, rather on the order of the way in which radical fundamentalist Christianity is the emphasized course of study in such American home-school curriculums as Gothard's Advanced Training Institute.

The facts of the story are simply these: when Obama was a child, his mother married for a second time to an Indonesian man, who was a Muslim, and the small family moved to Indonesia, a largely Muslim country, where they lived from 1967 until 1971. For two of the four years the family lived there, Obama attended a Roman Catholic school and, in his last two years, he attended the Basuki school, a secular public school or—as schools are known in that part of the world—a madrassa.

A now-defunct print and online magazine called *Insight on the News* that had been owned by News World Communications, which also owns the conservative *Washington Times*, ran a story that claimed then-Senator Obama had attended a radical Islamic school *when he was six years old*. The story was shortly debunked by various news sources, including CNN which dispatched Senior International Correspondent John Vause to Jakarta to investigate. Vause subsequently reported on CNN's "The Situation Room": "I came here to Barack Obama's elementary school in Jakarta looking for what some are calling an Islamic madrassa... like the ones that teach hate and violence in Pakistan and Afghanistan. I've been to those madrassas in Pakistan... this school is nothing like that." Indeed, the school respected various religious traditions and welcomed students of all faiths, and its students dressed in neat uniforms while its teachers dressed in the western style.

The facts, as usual, didn't keep the right-wing from running with the story, however, and amplifying it through the power of their echo chamber.[81] In one story they managed to smear both Democratic campaigns, which required that both Democratic candidates for president refute it—a task that wasn't off the Obama campaign's to-do list for over a year. Fox News, in particular, was "unwilling to stop when they knew they were wrong or correct what they knew was a lie," says Robert Gibbs, Obama's communications director.

Though President Obama did, indeed, embrace the Christianity of the grandparents who raised him, there is something deeply unpatriotic and pitiful in a country where the Constitution includes a clause that there is no religious test for a candidate to hold office that the candidate was forced to defend his religious background.[82] But let's face it, the othering of Barack Obama began early in his first presidential race in two powerfully if frustratingly persistent ways. A mid-April 2008 CBS/*New York Times* survey found that 45% of registered Republicans believed the president had not been born in the U.S.—and in 2011, another CBS poll found that one in four Americans still believed Obama was foreign born. Even more bewildering is that, according to a 2010 Pew Research Center poll, 18% of Americans—a full one in five—*still* believe Obama is a Muslim.

THERE HAVE BEEN more overtly racist attacks on President Obama and his family over the course of their eight years in the White House. The depictions of the president with a full set of gold grills and neck chains, or eating a watermelon labeled as 'the flesh and blood of America," or the photo-shopped image of him and his wife as creatures from *Planet of the Apes*. And there are images that are intended to be even more demeaning. What the images all have in common, however, is that they're crude and I don't mean that in the sense that they're inexpertly drawn or otherwise amateurishly executed. On the contrary, some of them come with excellent production values. What I mean is that they represent a rudimentary and uncensored racism of the sort that might appeal to actors in the base of the party but that would be unseemly for a player on the national political stage to embrace. The face of public racism is, in these early days of the 21st century, more subtle, and therefore subversive. These days it would be unseemly for pundits and politicians to come right out and call Obama the n-word; instead, they couch their racism in concerns that he was not "natural born" or that his Arabic middle name, Hussein, is "troublesome."[83]

A Long History, Not Over Yet

> **"**Race doesn't really exist for you because it has never been a barrier. Black folks don't have that choice. **"**

Chimamanda Ngozi Adichie, Americanah

What is Racism?

According to the Merriam-Webster Online Dictionary, racism is "a belief that race is the primary determinant of human traits and capacities and that racial differences produce an inherent superiority of a particular race."

That's a short and straightforward, simplistic and not particularly enlightening definition.

The first objection is easy, with the key word: *belief.* The same source defines "belief" as "a feeling of being sure that someone or something exists or that something is true; a feeling that something is good, right, or valuable; a feeling of trust in the worth or ability of someone." One *believes* in God, that one's garden will flourish after it is planted, that one's team will make it to the playoffs. With rare exception do we *believe*—do we put our faith in—unpleasant or evil enterprises: that cruel and unusual punishment is good, that sexism is right, that holding the mindset we are doomed to failure before we even begin is valuable. Words matter and the use of this particular word within a definition of racism is careless, at best, and, at worst, underscores an outlook that racism is a benign phenomenon, or perhaps even a valid personal decision.

LET'S TRY FOR something a little more helpful for this conversation: Racism is a fetid concoction made up of bigotry, antagonism, stereotyping, discrimination, intolerance, and systematic emotional, economic, educational, and social cruelty and subjugation directed at someone of a different ethnicity in order to distinguish that ethnicity as inferior to one's own. It is not a "belief", it is a character flaw; it is most certainly not benign; and it does not consist solely of the overt sort of racism—verbal slurs and separate drinking fountains—that was made either socially unacceptable or outright illegal about fifty years ago in the United States.

While I would never say that the accomplishments of half a century ago were not good and necessary—indeed, they were revolutionary and helped to indubitably bend the moral arc of the universe toward justice—I do think we have to acknowledge two downsides to them. First, rather than being rightfully understood as the first step in addressing and correcting over four hundred years of racial oppression in this country, the accomplishments of the Civil Rights Era allowed some people—and I am talking here specifically about people who did not experience racial oppression as part of their everyday lives, as part and parcel of their skin color—to believe that President Lyndon Johnson scribbled out racism, both historical and forever into the future, with the stroke of a pen—and that the presidential election of Barack Obama is evidence this is a correct view. Significant as the Civil Rights legislation was in this case, it served the unintended consequence of stopping much of the conversation that the country was having about race in the 1960s.

The second downside is a direct result of that stunted conversation. With the passage of the Civil Rights Act in 1964, and the Voting Rights Act in 1965, and the subsequent, overarching idea that the country had now achieved racial equality, came disappointment on the part of the white populace that Blacks weren't able to immediately overcome the struggles we faced in joining the mainstream, middle class. R. M. MacIver, a Scottish sociologist, famously said, "Law cannot prescribe morality." It also cannot magically disappear centuries of economic, educational, political, and social disenfranchisement. We'll get into the particulars of these exclusions in detail in the coming paragraphs, but here we need to recognize that the continuing, post-Civil Rights Era-struggles of Blacks to achieve the parity made more possible with the Civil Rights legislation of the 1960s had the effect of reinforcing negative racial stereotypes in the minds of many white Americans. Those whose prejudices were hard-wired could find an easy excuse for their bigotry in the on-going inability of Black Americans, as a whole, to "make it", but even self-identified liberal whites could find themselves coming up short with an explanation of why Blacks were still unable to make the leap into the middle class. Maybe Blacks *were* lazy, less intelligent and ambitious and morally different? Perhaps the culture really was broken—like their *homes*—and it led them, particularly young African-American men, to reject education and gravitate toward street life, violence and vice?[84]

This is why it is critical that we pick up the thread of the conversation where it left off in the Civil Rights Era if we want to understand how we got to where we are today. We need to stop focusing on now-socially unacceptable racial slurs and now-illegal separate drinking fountains as touchstones of racism and start taking aim at the more insidious ways that institutional racism was—and continues to be—manifested. Burning crosses and white hoods are still terrifying; however, the broader public now understands them as the marks of an angry, resentful militant extremist tribal cohort. And Jim Crow may have been abolished; however, the attributes of it persist and the structural disadvantages it locked into law linger—to be sure when the courts, in 2016, still have to throw out laws passed within the last few years by state legislatures like North Carolina, and signed by the state's governor, that the court outright acknowledges was intended overtly to specifically disenfranchise Black voters, Jim Crow still very much lives in spirit and in actual law wherever it finds place to root. Clearly the only thing stopping state legislatures from trying to block the political rights of Black people today are still, in fact, the Civil Rights laws passed by the Federal government many

years ago; not a compass belief in the basic ethos of Democracy in which they claim to have faith, not a change
of conscience, not a moral re-evaluation, but simply the
law. You might think the basic right to vote upon which
group political power rests and the heart of our Democracy lives would now be a given that we have long since
passed having to fight for or discuss, but clearly you would
be wrong because the only thing that has changed in this
space has been the laws, not the nature of tribalism. So the
moment the laws holding back the worst structural ten-
ants of tribalism are lifted in America, real racism, not the
name-calling, but the *real* racist ghost whose sole intent is
the retention of power rattles its chains once more. I tire so
of the continued refrain about how far we've come—and I
ask: what cause does this refrain work for? Post-racial, indeed. We cannot be post-racial because power is always
imminent and reaching toward the future.

Redlining, and All That Follows

The practice known as "redlining" began with the National Housing Act of 1934, a New Deal effort to help
make home mortgages more affordable and stem the tide
of housing foreclosures during the Great Depression. As
part of this program, the FHA (Federal Housing Administration) created what it called "residential security maps"
for over two hundred U.S. cities to be used as guides for
banks and other lenders to determine if a property was a
good or a risky investment.

The city in question was divided into four distinct areas. Areas which were generally populated by "American Business and Professional Men" were considered great locations, and safe risks, for lenders, and were shaded in the map in green. Areas that were less desirable, but that the map makers considered stable, were shaded in blue. Areas that were declining—based on the quality of the homes, the sparcity of residents, or if they bordered even less desireable areas—were shaded in yellow. Areas in which decline had already taken place, and that were populated by low income families, were shaded in red—and it is this shading from which the term "redlining" derives.

While racial segregation certainly existed before the FHA's guidelines went into effect, "residential security maps" institutionalized the practice. How? Well, the wealth gap between Black families and white families is nothing new. In 1934, the median annual income for a white household was about $1500.[85] For Black households it was $474.[86] When the folks at the FHA took out their crayons to shade in a map, it was pretty obvious what color an area was going to be based on the color of the skin of its residents. These maps also charted a course to this injustice: affluent Black families were often denied mortgages based on where they chose to make their homes, while lower-income white families qualified based on their blue district locations. Indeed, of the over 120 billion dollars in federal home-owner subsidies that were disbursed between 1934 and 1962, only 2% went to families of color.[87]

It wasn't only banks, however, that used the FHA's maps to do, or not to do, business. Insurance agencies based their decisions on whether or not to offer policies to a customer based on where his or her home was located on the map. Hospitals decided where to build or expand based on a location's proximity to the most desirable—green or blue—areas of the map. Retail stores, including supermarkets, chose their locations based on the disposable income of their potential customers, in green or blue districts—the beginnings of what we, today, call "food deserts".

The lack of or, in best-case scenarios, inconvenience to vital services was but one of the fallouts of redlining. In this country, property taxes are what fund our schools; people who live in neighborhoods with lower property values have to send their kids to substandard schools where the equipment and books are outdated or insufficient, the teachers are overburdened with large class sizes, and/or the buildings themselves are often in disrepair. When children attend schools where it is challenging to get the best education, their ability to qualify for high-paying jobs or compete for a place in a college program are undermined. Additionally, while as of this writing most wealth in this country is not inherited,[88] a majority of us can expect to inherit from our parents the proceeds from what is for most middle-class people their greatest asset, their home, when they pass on. Because of redlining, generations of people of color have had no homes, or have had homes of lesser value, to pass on and assist the next generation in accumulating wealth. The fallout from this disparity continues to be felt today. According to the Pew Research Center, as of 2008, 74.9% of whites own their own homes, but only 48.9% of Hispanics, and 47.5% of Blacks own their own homes.

You might be surprised to learn that, in spite of the 1968 Fair Housing Act and the 1988 Fair Housing amendments, a form of redlining still goes on today. Realtors still engage in what is called "racial steering"—keeping neighborhoods segregated by showing clients homes only in areas where a majority of people of the same race live. According to that same Pew Research Center report, predatory lenders target minority groups: "In 2007, 27.6% of home purchase loans to Hispanics and 33.5% to Blacks were higher-priced loans, compared with just 10.5 % of home purchase loans to whites that year. For black homeowners who had a higher-priced mortgage, the typical annual percentage rate (APR) was about 3 percentage points greater than the rate on a typical 30-year, fixed-rate conventional mortgage..." It was as recently as 2015, as a matter of fact, that the Department of Housing and Urban Development (HUD) declared victory in "one of the largest redlining complaints" ever brought by the federal government against a mortgage lender. That lender was Associated Bank, headquartered in Wisconsin, which settled claims that it discriminated from 2008 through 2010 against Black and Hispanic borrowers.[89] It perhaps goes without saying, then, that minorities have been among the hardest hit by the on-going foreclosure crisis, but take this for a concrete example: in Cleveland, Ohio, the site of 2016's Republican Convention, Jim Rokakis, the vice president of the Western Reserve Land Conservancy and director of the Thriving Communities Institute, estimates that, in that city alone, African-American and Latino households have suffered an approximate combined one-trillion-dollar loss in home values.[90]

Lest you begin to consider that redlining, insidious as it was and is, is the *only* factor that has influenced the trajectory of structural racism in this country, let me point out two more institutional examples of it. First, when the U.S. Congress created Social Security in 1935, as a safety net for its citizens, the provisions of the act explicitly excluded domestic and agricultural workers—jobs held predominantly at the time by Mexican, Asian, and African-American workers. These were low-paying jobs, so these were the people who were least able to save for retirement or a rainy day, yet they were completely shut off from the safety net. Second, again in 1935, Congress passed the Wagner Act, which legalized labor organizing—but nonwhites were specifically excluded from it. This meant that high-paying union jobs, and the benefits of medical care and job security that went along with them, were denied to nonwhites—an exclusion that lasted well into the 1970s!

WHILE YOUNGER BLACKS are still coping with the fallout from these sorts of systematic, institutional impediments that were placed in the way of their parents, grandparents, great-grandparents and even older generations, they are also dealing with the day-to-day injuries inflicted by the still-entrenched biases of the waning power structure.

Some of the manifestations of those prejudices are "merely" humiliating. Maybe it's a thug who attacks children with racial slurs.[91] Maybe it's some clueless college coed approaching a group of Black and Hispanic kids on a recruitment tour of her college campus and asking them if they like her Confederate flag earrings.[92] Maybe it's not getting a call back for a job interview because he or she has a "Black-sounding" name.[93] As the President himself said, when speaking to the American people on the day George Zimmerman's verdict was handed down for the 2012 murder of Trayvon Martin: "There are very few African-American men in this country who haven't had the experience of being followed when they were shopping in a department store. That includes me. And there are very few African-American men who haven't had the experience of walking across the street and hearing the locks click on the doors of cars. That happens to me, at least before I was a senator. There are very few African-Americans who haven't had the experience of getting on an elevator and a woman clutching her purse nervously and holding her breath until she had a chance to get off. That happens often. And, you know, I—I don't want to exaggerate this, but those sets of experiences inform how the African-American community interprets what happened one night in Florida. And it's inescapable for people to bring those experiences to bear."

Some of the prejudices are fatal. Ask Trayvon Martin's parents. Or Michael Brown's. Or Tamir Rice's.

I'm the father of two sons, two young Black men, and I have taught them that, when we are out on the streets of Washington, D.C., the city where we live and in which I work, they are not allowed to horse around, or goof off, or run. Because too often when a police officer sees a young Black man running, his first thought isn't, "That kid looks like he's having fun," it's, "What's he running away from? What crime has he committed?"

If you are Black in America—particularly if you are a Black *man*—you already understand why I counsel my sons in this way. People of color are vastly more likely to be stopped for "looking suspicious" than Whites who, in many cases, are doing the same thing or behaving in a similar way—in other words, they are profiled. For example, in New York City, in 2009, just over half a million people were stopped by the police; even though people of color make up approximately 50% of the population of the city, a full 84% of people detained by police that year were people of color.[94]

According to Bureau of Justice statistics, Black drivers are 13% more likely to be pulled over in traffic than white drivers—though, depending on the city, that number can go as high as 26%.[95]

When an arrest is made, those charged with a crime are tried under laws that target people of color. For example, powdered cocaine is typically used by more affluent and whiter drug users, and crack cocaine is typically used by minorities and those in lower income brackets.[96] The sentencing guidelines for those convicted of possession of crack cocaine are wildly disproportionate, however, to the guidelines for possession of powder cocaine—18:1.[97] That is, a person caught with one gram of crack cocaine is looking at the same sentence as a person caught with eighteen grams of powder cocaine. This in spite of the fact that an estimated 12% of the U.S. population uses powder cocaine and only 4% uses crack cocaine.[98] But could it be that this is all just the unintended consequences of America trying to make its streets safe? Of policy makers just trying to, in fact, enact the best policies to solve the problem?

In March of 2016, an interview with John Ehrlichman, a key figure in the Watergate scandal of the early 1970s, was published after twenty-two years. In this interview, Ehrlichman admitted at long last that the Nixon administration's crackdown on drugs was really a war on anti-war hippies and Blacks. "You understand what I'm saying?" Erlichman asked in the interview. "We knew we couldn't make it illegal to be either against the war or black, but by getting the public to associate the hippies with marijuana and blacks with heroin. And then criminalizing both heavily, we could disrupt those communities. We could arrest their leaders, raid their homes, break up their meetings, and vilify them night after night on the evening news. Did we know we were lying about the drugs? Of course we did."[99] Forty-plus years and counting, these sorts of laws are doing exactly what they were, and are, intended to do—disempower the Black community. The predicate for the war on drugs was not safer streets and less drug use (we certainly haven't gotten that); no, the predicate was to dilute Black power and keep communities of color weakened and dependent.

Which leads us directly into the issue of mass incarceration. In the 1980s, America's prisons began to be widely privatized,[100] and the number of people who were incarcerated exploded—from about half a million to 2.3 million—and African-Americans and Hispanics make up nearly 60% of that prison population. Black men are incarcerated at six times the rate of white men, which, if you compare that statistic with population figures, means that one in six Black men has spent time in prison—and, if the trend continues, it will mean that one in three Black males born today can expect to spend time in prison in his lifetime.[101]

This does not mean that Black men are six times more criminally inclined than white men; it does mean that Black communities are policed more harshly, Blacks can expect to be picked up for "looking suspicious" more routinely, and Blacks can expect tougher sentences when convicted of a crime. Let's go back a paragraph and talk about America's drug problem again: it has been estimated that 14 million whites are users of illegal drugs, and 2.6 million Blacks are users—five times as many whites are using illegal drugs as Blacks, yet African-Americans are sent to prison for drug-related crimes at ten times the rate of whites.[102]

What about time off for good behavior? Determining an amount for a defendant's bond? Assessing a prisoner's future rehabilitation needs? The computer algorithms used in justice departments' risk-assessment software is biased against Black defendants—and in 2014 then-U.S. Attorney General Eric Holder called for the U.S. Sentencing Commission to do a thorough study of their use "to ensure individualized and equal justice." The Commission declined.[103]

At the end of the day, however, too often a suspect may never get a chance to answer the initial question "What's he running away from?" at all. According to the most recent reporting to the FBI, over the seven-year period 2005 to 2012, white cops killed two Black people a *week*—though the FBI admits their database is flawed and incomplete: not all police departments participate in reporting so the actual number of deaths is likely higher.[104]

WHILE SUBSTANDARD HOUSING, inferior education, racial profiling, racially targeted laws, and mass incarceration are huge problems in the U.S., they're not, of course, the only systemic impediments that people of color face. For example, an estimated twenty million more people have health insurance today than they did before Obamacare, but, according to Lisa A. Cooper, MD, MPH, and a professor in the Division of General Internal Medicine at the Johns Hopkins School of Medicine, "It's been really extensively shown that minorities don't receive the same quality of health care as whites in the United States."[105] A study published in the *American Journal of Public Health* found that two-thirds of doctors harbored "unconscious" racial biases which resulted in slower speech speed when visiting with African-American patients, physician-dominated dialogue, lower levels of patient-centeredness…and lower levels of positive emotional tone in contrast to visits with white patients."[106] The patients, as a result, were less involved in determining treatment options, less apt to follow through with recommended care, and less able to control diseases such as diabetes and depression.[107]

The impediments are huge, entrenched, and around every corner.

Yet when a movement begins that seeks to dismantle these impediments, it nearly always crashes into opposition. The latest is Black Lives Matter, "an ideological and political intervention in a world where Black lives are systematically and intentionally targeted for demise. It is an affirmation of Black folks' contributions to this society, our humanity, and our resilience in the face of deadly oppression."[108] It is a movement that embraces guiding principles[109] as broad and humane as you could hope to find even among people who weren't as thirsty for justice—which is why it is hard not to come to the conclusion that pundits and others who push back against it[110] have either not read those principles, or have more sinister if, perhaps, unconscious fears surrounding the self-empowerment of the country's Black population.

Let's look at two events that happened relatively close together. On April 12, 2014, a group of armed protestors advanced on United States Bureau of Land Management agents who were clearing Cliven Bundy's illegally grazing cattle from federal lands in southeastern Nevada—the Bureau's solution to a twenty-year legal dispute during which Bundy had paid no grazing fees. The Bureau's newly-confirmed director, Neil Kornze, elected to release the cattle that had already been rounded up, in order to de-escalate the stand-off, and Bundy remained free—continuing to graze his cattle, for free, on federal land—until February 10, 2016, when he tried to join armed militants in yet another Bundy-led standoff with federal agents at the Malheur National Wildlife Refuge. In between stand-offs, Cliven Bundy had a brief fling as a folk hero thanks to extensive air time and incessant promotion by Fox News, until he went on a racial tirade even the folks at Fox News couldn't stomach: "I want to tell you one more thing I know about the Negro. When I go to Las Vegas, north Las Vegas, and I would see these little Government houses, and in front of that Government house the door was usually open, and the older people and the kids and there was always at least half a dozen people on the porch. They didn't have nothing to do, they didn't have nothing for the kids to do, they didn't have nothing for the young girls to do. They were basically on government subsidy, so now what do they do? They abort their young children, they put their young men in jail, because they never learned how to pick cotton. And I've often wondered, are they better off as slaves, picking cotton and having a family life and doing things, or are they better off under government subsidy? They didn't get no more freedom. They got less freedom."[111] The crucial part of this story is that conservative pundits made Cliven Bundy, a man who had gotten away with stealing from the U.S. government for over two decades, their darling for engaging in armed conflict with agents of the federal government.

When it came to events in Ferguson, Missouri a few months later, neither the police nor the pundits were quite as generous with a group of people who, peacefully and sorrowfully, pushed back when one of their number was murdered by law enforcement. Ferguson was already a textbook town in terms of how much more harshly its Black population was policed versus its white population,[112] before the night of August 9, 2014, when Police Officer Darren Wilson shot and killed an unarmed teenager, Michael Brown. In response, local law enforcement reacted to the peaceful memorial observance of the community by sending out a hundred and fifty officers in riot gear—and one of the officers allowed a dog who was under his control to urinate on flowers in the makeshift memorial.[113] Police cars trampled more flower arrangements and candles.[114] "That made people in the crowd mad," said Missouri state representative Sharon Pace, "and it made me mad."[115] The contempt for the grief and despair of the community was stunning, but it was the militarization of the police response that escalated the situation.[116] Indeed, the widespread criticism of police tactics used in Ferguson were what led Senator Claire McCaskill (D-MI), chairwoman of the Homeland Security and Governmental Affairs' Financial and Contracting Oversight subcommittee, to hold hearings to probe the militarization of local police departments.

The right wing, however, labeled the calls of the people of Ferguson for redress as, incredibly, "lynch-mob justice."[117] And then they did one more thing that they routinely do when they want to dismiss a criminal act for what it is, and justify its commission: they decided the victim was "no angel."

Blaming the victim is nothing new, of course. In the case of rape, women have been subjected to it for millennia, and have been actively fighting back against it for at least half a century, battle-wearied from having to deal with politicians who promote the concept of "legitimate rape"[118] or judges who coddle rapists because they buy the excuse of "party culture."[119]

Similarly, you can set a stopwatch to calculate how

quickly conservative pundits will find an excuse to make a victim of a police shooting culpable for his or her own death. Michael Brown shoplifted from a convenience store! Eric Garner was hustling loose cigarettes! Sandra Bland was uncooperative! Trayvon Martin was wearing provocative attire!

It is important to break down and bottom line what the Right Wing is actually saying when they engage in these verbal gymnastics to justify to the rest of us a crime they're actually comfortable with. What they're saying is Black people who sell loose cigarettes, or have the audacity to want to know why they're being arrested, or wear hoodies deserve to die.[120]

But race has, in this country, historically allowed for a double standard. I have, for example, recently heard gun-control proponents discuss with disgust and frustration how quickly congressional Republicans would jump on the gun-control bandwagon if those open-carry advocates who stroll around supermarkets, through big box stores, and down city streets with their rifles slung over their shoulders or holsters buckled to their hips were not white. You can almost hear the glee in their voices as they imagine the wide-eyed fear on Paul Ryan's face as he scrambled to gavel Congress into session to cast its votes in favor of background checks and "No Fly, No Buy" if it were Black people taking to the streets with weapons strapped to their backs.

These folks have no idea how very right they are. Possibly the last time a Republican was enthusiastic about gun control, and eager to pass laws to enact it, was on May

2, 1967—when about thirty young Black people climbed the steps of California's capitol building, loaded with .357 Magnums, 12-gauge shotguns, and .45-caliber pistols. At the top of the steps, Black Panther Bobby Seale read from a prepared statement: "The American people in general and the black people in particular, must take careful note of the racist California legislature aimed at keeping the black people disarmed and powerless. Black people have begged, prayed, petitioned, demonstrated, and everything else to get the racist power structure of America to right the wrongs which have historically been perpetuated against black people The time has come for black people to arm themselves against this terror before it is too late."[121]

The Mulford Act of 1967, named for Republican California state congressman Don Mulford and which repealed open carry in the state, was crafted for the express purpose of disarming the Black Panthers. Ronald Reagan, then California's governor and who was present at the state capitol when the Panthers arrived with their shotguns and pistols, said he saw "no reason why on the street today a citizen should be carrying loaded weapons," before signing the Mulford Act into law.

Sadly, as I was writing this passage, I got a text message on my phone from the organization Color of Change: "With the death of #AltonSterling police are on pace to kill 1 Black person every day in 2016." Why did Alton Sterling have to die? Because as he was selling bootleg CDs—and because, when police had him restrained and immobilized on the ground, someone shouted "Gun."

The very next morning I woke up to the news of the

murder of Philando Castile in the St. Paul, Minnesota suburb of Falcon Heights. Why did Castile have to die? Because the tail light on his car was broken—and because as he was reaching for the license and registration that the arresting officer had asked him to produce, Castile was explaining that he also had a *licensed* pistol in the car.[122]

Let me state this as clearly as possible: Louisiana is an open-carry state. Minnesota allows concealed carry. Conservative pundits jumped on the fact that both Alton Sterling and Philando Castile were in the possession and/or proximity of guns at the time of their murders—and what I want to know is where is conservative outrage that two U.S. citizens were murdered while exercising their legal right to bear arms?

YET TODAY MANY of us manage to flourish even in the face of institutional racism. It is these examples that those opposed to civil rights and other conservatives will serve up to "prove" that there is no such thing as institutional racism. If there were such a thing, they argue, then we would not have any examples of successful Blacks—Brown University president Ruth Simmons, Nobel Prize-winning author Toni Morrison, Supreme Court Justice Clarence Thomas, Oprah Winfrey, Michael Jordan, President Barack Obama! Indeed, according to a study by the *Journal of Personality and Social Psychology*, "incidental exposure to a Black person who is 'successful in a nonstereotypical setting'" is just exactly what makes people more likely to believe that institutional racism is a thing of the past.[123]

What these people are doing is called "individuating."

On November 1, 1945, Branch Rickey, president and general manager of the Brooklyn Dodgers, signed Jackie Robinson, breaking the color line in American professional baseball. Rickey purposefully chose Robinson, knowing that his unquestionable talent would put to rest the conventional excuses that formed the basis for the sport's traditional segregation policy, and that his temperament would allow him to withstand the foreordained racial insults that would come when he took the field. Robinson had also attended UCLA, served honorably in the armed forces during WWII, and was a married man and a father who loved his wife and kids. The man who integrated the major leagues could not be only Black, he had to have both the background and the fortitude to withstand the abuse that surely would be thrown his way.

Rosa Parks was not a tired seamstress, too weary to give up her seat on a bus. She had a high school degree—at a time when only about 15% of African-American women had one,[124] was happily married, and was a long-time civil rights activist. The woman who kept her seat on the bus could not be only Black but could carry not one whiff of scandal about her.

Barack Obama is supremely well educated, a former constitutional professor, and a loving husband and doting father. He carried with him not a trace of ethical scandal, and no instances where he could be aligned closely with typical Black stereotypes. He worked his ass off to get through an Ivy League school and, instead of taking his degree and going off with it to Wall Street, as he well could have done, he chose to become a community organizer and give something back to his community. The man who became our first Black president could not be only Black—he had to be an exceptional individual who sparked the hope and imagination of the American people, and who was in line with the values of the majority, and who *happened* to be Black.

Our society has largely individuated people like Michael Jordan or Oprah Winfrey. To a certain extent, they aren't first and foremost just Black, they are individuals. If you're Black and not individuated, you're just plain Black—unknown to them, anonymous, a nameless Joe Blow. As Joe Blow you carry all the stereotypes associated with your group—you're dangerous and less ethical. You're a plain Black guy on the street, you reach for your wallet and, for all they know it could be a gun because you are, of course, dangerous by way of your blackness. This strangeness gives them the right to empty their clip into us.

IN THE 2008 election it was Sarah Palin's job—likely one she took upon herself, judging from Senator McCain's obvious discomfort with the fallout from her rogue enterprise[125]—to *un*individuate Barack Obama. Dissonant to progressive ears was her charge that he was a *mere* community organizer. That the then-Democratic nominee had, as I've already pointed out, taken his Ivy League degree and headed not to Wall Street but back into the community to help others spoke to something important about this values that resonated with us: he was not selfish, not self-serving;

his heart was truly a servant's. This same selflessness, however, was one of the character traits for which those on the right sought to vilify him. Some progressives I've spoken to about the dissonance this caused for us put it down to an attempt not to malign his life experience, but rather to other the candidate's loyalties: he doesn't understand capitalism, he doesn't care about making money, *he doesn't understand the American way of life*—he's a foreigner, a Muslim, "I am just so fearful that this is not a man who sees America the way that you and I see America, as the greatest source for good in this world. I'm afraid this is someone who sees America as imperfect enough to work with a former domestic terrorist who targeted his own country."[126]

Let's forget for the moment the terrorists Palin was palin' around with[127] before her ill-fated leap onto the national stage, and focus, again, on her purpose in such attacks: to make Senator Obama scary; to make him seem as if he is not one of us. In 2012, in the midst of Romney's unsuccessful bid to unseat President Obama, the Republicans doubled down on this strategy—from which one could draw a direct line to the fact that the 2016 Republican nominee is the most prominent "birther" of all.

In their attempts to "other" Barack Obama to the point of raising fear of him in the American people, the Republicans succeeded—and they failed, too. How you read these numbers will depend on whether you're a glass-half-full or a glass-half-empty sort of person: in 2008 the McCain/Palin campaign garnered 55% of the white vote, to Obama's 43%[128]; and in 2012, the Romney/Ryan campaign garnered 59% of the white vote, to Obama's 39%.[129] Among voting blocs broken down in these reports—women, Blacks, Hispanics, the LGBT community, etc.—these attempts to "other" the Democratic candidate were successful, but they didn't count on the continued increases in voting by non-whites as, indeed, in 2012 the African- American became the most likely voter in the country. Tribalism in 2012, and very likely in every national Presidential election to come, is and will increasingly become an electoral receipt for GOP disaster. And they know as much; their infamous "autopsy report" following the 2012 election loss states as much. As the demographics continue to move us toward a majority minority country and minorities, particularly African-American voters, keep pace and outpace white turnout rates, it's hard to understand how the Republican Party's almost exclusive white tribal organizing philosophy will win them the future. Yet, here we are, in 2016, with Donald Trump doubling down on racial resentment and expanding the Southern Strategy as a pathway to the White House. At the center of his campaign strategy has to be the idea that, frankly, while Romney bested even the great Ronald Reagan, Trump will be able to go even further in running up the percentage of the white vote simply by overtly playing to tribalism in a way no Republican nominee in modern times has dared do—or, perhaps, more importantly, seemingly thought was best. His campaign strategy is, to my mind, the most cynical of any in modern American history.

AND THAT THOUGHT—Black people voting—brings us neatly to the final topics that we need to discuss in this chapter—the latest hypocritical wielding power tools: the recent push to restrict voters of color from exercising their franchise, and the gerrymandering of election districts to skew election results to the white Right.

Any discussion of the recent spate of voter restriction laws needs to begin with a simple disclaimer: voter fraud, the crime these laws are supposed to address, is a myth. In a comprehensive study, one analyst, writing for the *Washington Post*, was able to discover only thirty-one instances of voter fraud in the period from 2000 through 2014, out of more than *one billion* votes cast in that same period nationwide—and the investigator believes that many of those thirty-one "fraudulent" votes will turn out, as have so many other such claims, to be matters of clerical errors: "a problem with matching people from one big computer list to another, or a data entry error, or confusion between two different people with the same name, or someone signing in on the wrong line of a pollbook."[130] To put that into perspective, contrast the number of potentially fraudulent votes, thirty-one, against the three thousand votes which, in just four states, in general elections alone, have been affirmatively rejected by election boards for lack of appropriate ID, and you begin to see the makings of real voter fraud: enough legitimate voters turned away from the polls that election results are altered.

The reasonable questions that follow are: Who are the people who are promoting these tougher voter restriction laws, and why do they want to alter the results of U.S. elections?

Since 2010 and the midterm elections in which Tea Party candidates were swept into national, state, and local elected office, at least 180 restrictive voting laws in forty-one states have been introduced in legislative sessions— each and every one of them introduced by Republicans.

Keep that in mind as we discuss our next topic, gerrymandering

Every ten years since 1790, in all years ending with a zero, a census is taken in the United States. Among the purposes the census serves is to keep the United States House of Representatives apportioned appropriately. Based on data gathered in the census, the boundaries of elective districts are redrawn to maintain equal representation on the basis of population. Gerrymandering is the practice of using the decennial event of the census to manipulate the boundaries of electoral districts in order to gain or create a partisan advantage in that district. As *Rolling Stone* noted, GOP donors poured cash into Republican races across state lines in the lead-up to the 2010 midterm elections precisely because 2010 was a census year[131]—precisely because the party that is in the majority in a census year has a lot of sway in determining the boundaries of election districts as they are redrawn to accommodate updated population data. As a result of the 2010 midterm elections and its GOP sweep, election districts have been redrawn in the U.S. with boundaries that will benefit the Republican party at least through the 2020 elections—and the way these districts have been redrawn reflect some of the most brazenly egregious gerrymandering the U.S. has ever endured.

To understand what was done, let's look at the congressional election results from the 2012 election. That year a popular president was up for reelection, which can drive voter turnout and, indeed, President Obama beat Mitt Romney with 51.1% of the popular vote to Romney's 47.2%—the first president since Eisenhower in the 1950s to crack 51% two elections in a row! He won twenty-six states, and a total of 332 Electoral College votes! He carried down ballot Democratic candidates on his broad coattails and these candidates scored nearly 1.4 million more votes than Republican candidates—and, because this was what the people said they wanted when they spoke at the ballot box, the House of Representatives, "the people's house," went blue once again…!

Right?

Well, no spoilers here, the House remained red after the 2012 election. That election was the first one since the 2010 redistricting, and the country's electoral maps were gerrymandered to help protect and entrench the GOP majority/the white majority regardless of how many more votes nationally the other party won. In spite of the will of the people of America, the majority of which voted for a Democratic candidate, Congress remained reliably in the hands of the Republican Party—minority rule.

Now to be fair, gerrymandering isn't new and both sides certainly have tried to take advantage and create districts that protect incumbents, but now the science of it is different. With sophisticated voter files and mathematical voter models we can gerrymander perfectly, right down to the block and house level within precincts. We have gerrymandered real competition out of the majority of our congressional districts and thus lost the U.S. Congress as an actual representative body that will in turn reflect the will of the people. This is how Democracy is lost—to a computer model.

As demographic changes continue to unsettle our political grounds, protecting and perpetuating tribal power becomes paramount. Voter suppression laws and the gerrymandering of districts at both the federal and state level are central tactics of those who would cling to a tribal-power vision of America. Some on the right might think of these tactics as very clever ways to maintain the status quo in the face of radically changing national demographics, and may even be wholly unashamed of their part in the process,[132] but the rest of us cannot afford to look the other way and let them get away with their deluded sense of patriotism. For, surely, if there's anything that conservatives like to do, it's wrap themselves up in their misunderstanding of what it means to be a patriot.

Voting rights in America—particularly voting rights for particular groups of people: Blacks, women, youth over eighteen but under twenty-one years of age—have been in contention since the founding of the country. With each passing year—or decade, or, in some cases, century, however, legislation has been passed that enfranchised more and more of her citizens. That more wholly embraced the constitutional amendments—specifically the 15th, 19th, and 26th—which prohibit voting rights from being abridged on account of race, sex, age, or other conditions such as previous servitude. Though individual states have attempted tactics in the past to restrict voting—poll taxes during Jim Crow, for example, that indirectly kept racial minorities from casting ballots—these tactics had been systematically and progressively struck down in favor of enfranchisement.

But in the midterm elections of 2014, American voters faced voting ID laws that were regressive for the first time since Reconstruction.

I call bullshit on phony patriots who think they're being anything but anti-American and racist by finding novel ways to prohibit people from exercising their right to vote. You cannot make it deliberately more difficult for people to vote at the same time that you call yourself a lover of constitutional ideals. When you deny your fellow citizens their rights and privileges under the law, you lose the right to call yourself a true American. And indeed when you want to win not by competing best in a free market of ideas, but instead by gaming the system to determine winners and losers, you strike me as a communist instead of someone who loves and believes in Democracy.

You cannot think of yourself as someone grounded in the principals of capitalism if you engage in these regulations and manipulations that keep voters from casting ballots, or make their votes meaningless because their election districts are so unbalanced. Your free market ideas can't start and stop at Wall Street. If you truly believe in the ideas of the free market, then you are bound by your ideas to put your best products into the marketplace and allow them to compete—and then live with the outcome. But if you feel the need to go through any manner of gyrations to rig the marketplace—or the polling place—that can only be because you understand that your ideas can't compete on a level playing field and you're gaming the system to decide winners and losers.

When Racism Becomes Treason

" The Nation has not yet found peace from its sins; the freedman has not yet found freedom in his promised land. **"**

W. E. B. DuBois, The Souls of Black Folk

How does it feel to be a problem?

W. E. B. DuBois asked that question in 1903, in his seminal book, *The Souls of Black Folk.* The context of the question was the author's meetings with people of "the other world"—white people—who would often tell him about the "excellent colored man" who lived in their town, or volunteer that they had fought at Mechanicsville, or allude to "Southern outrages". They would reference subjects they believed he, as a Black man, might especially appreciate— thus acknowledging that he *was* a Black man and that they both knew of and approved another like him—but, at least in his presence, they tiptoed carefully around any honest discussion of race, or the real inquiry he felt they wanted to make: *How does it feel to be a problem?* It was a question DuBois felt his white acquaintances were too kind or too timid to frame but which he sought to answer anyway.

So let's honor DuBois and not tiptoe around the question either. Let's admit he was entirely right: racism, embodied by the people whose skin color sets them apart from what has long been the majority race, has presented a problem in America since the first nineteen slaves sailed to the new world on a Dutch trading ship and landed on the shining shores of Jamestown, Virginia, in 1619.

For the first two hundred and fifty years or so that Black people existed in North America, they existed as slaves, and so the first problem Black people posed for the American colonists was one of morality. While some scholars will demur that the Bible treats slavery as a social fact—which, in fact, in Biblical times it was—and therefore a sort of convention cultures had to outgrow as they matured, the religious community has long held that it was a depraved institution. As an example, the Roman Catholic church had long stood in opposition to it: St. Patrick, himself once a slave, denounced the institution in the fifth century; in 1102, when he was the Archbishop of Canterbury, St. Anselm oversaw an ecclesiastical council that prohibited the "nefarious trade" in England. Pope Eugene IV issued a papal bull ordering the emancipation of slaves in the newly colonized Canary Islands in 1435—a bull Pope Urban VIII upheld in 1639. In 1686 the Holy Office of the Inquisition issued an edict that held that the enslavement of Black Africans was immoral. Though by the mid-1800s many American Catholic clergy were contorting the instructions within papal bulls in order to provide divine cover for slaveholders, it was indeed religious fervor—in this case that of evangelical Christians in the midst of the Great Awakening—that undergirded the cause of the abolitionists and culminated in the Civil War.

On January 1, 1863, President Abraham Lincoln issued an executive order—the Emancipation Proclamation—an order that, as most high-school history classes teach, freed the slaves. It did not. Or, at least, it did not free all of them. It freed the slaves in states, or areas of states, where rebellion against the Union had already been subdued, and, as Union armies progressed, it freed the slaves in areas that came under Union control. Importantly, however, it did not free slaves in states that were neither in rebellion nor under Confederate control, such as Maryland, Delaware, Missouri, or Kentucky, or in other specified areas, such as certain counties of Virginia. In truth the abolition of slavery in the whole of the United States wouldn't happen until the Thirteenth Amendment to the Constitution passed Congress and was then ratified by the states—an act that wasn't accomplished until December 6, 1865. Even then, ex-slaves did not automatically become citizens of the United States but abided under the legally fluid term "freedmen".

More central to our discussion here is that Emancipation created a huge problem in and of itself. On the morning of January 2, 1863, four million former slaves did not wake up after a night of celebrating their new liberty and settle down into comfortable, middle-class lives. Rather, as the Civil War continued to rage, as more and more lands

were subdued by the Union forces, thousands of slaves—
hungry, ill-clothed, and frightened—descended each day
upon Union army encampments. Food and clean water
were in short supply; the South's infrastructure had been
destroyed in battle, and sanitation was deplorable and
growing worse with each new wave of refugees. It was a crisis, and it was left to the military to manage the immediate
needs of these displaced people, though no federal funds
were allocated for the purpose, and private philanthropy
was woefully disorganized.

In 1865, the Freedmen's Bureau was established. It was
an agency of the federal government that operated under
the Department of War, the only existing agency equipped
at the time to be assigned to the South, to assist these four
million newly-free people settle on land of their own, find
employment, learn to read and write—and the intent was
to accomplish this transition from a slave society within
one year, the length of time for which the agency was char-
tered. The intent was admirable, but funds were almost
non-existent, and the timeframe was optimistic, to say the
very least.

To this daunting scenario, factor in the disparities of
human nature. The South was not, as cliché would have
it, overrun with scoundrels during the time of Reconstruction—there were willing, capable, and well-intentioned
people who were part of the operation on behalf of both
the government and the private sector; indeed, the iconic
image we have of the New England schoolteacher took
form at this time as women from that region headed South
to set up schools for the now-legal task of educating Black

Americans—but there were, to paraphrase DuBois, just enough flies to ruin all of the ointment. Able-bodied African-American males were enlisted in the Union army, only to find that all too often their pay disappeared into the pockets of unscrupulous clerks before it could be handed over to them. The government initially set aside confiscated lands upon which former slaves could settle, build homes and begin farming, but the vast majority of this land was, instead, sold at a profit to whomever had the means to pay for it—and the former slaves did not have the means. Possibly the worst blow to a population struggling not just to earn a wage but to become *accustomed* to earning a wage and all matters of budgeting and saving that go along with that custom, was that, about ten years following Emancipation, the very banking institutions that had been set up to meet this need of the Freedmen went bankrupt. Nearly ten years of freely-accumulated Black wealth, the fruits of a decade of toil, was gone nearly overnight—and no one was prosecuted for the crime of mismanaging these financial institutions. The psychological blow to the community was devastating.

The hardest part, however, was a thing both less tangible and more dangerous. The newly freed were recreating their lives in the land of their former masters, in the midst of people still stinging from defeat and seething with resentment over their Lost Cause. In the wake of Emancipation, Southern whites who believed that for white men to live among free Blacks went against the natural order set about crafting ever-more creative and systematic ways to keep Blacks continually impoverished, politically

disenfranchised, and physically and psychologically intimidated. From the theft of their pay, to lynchings, to the separate water fountains and segregated schools and redlining
of the Jim Crow-era, to the more modern-day tactics of
voter restriction and gerrymandering, you can draw a
straight line through the evolving strategies each generation of the majority population has used to respond to the
problem of America's color line.

As we discussed earlier, however, America's demographics are rapidly changing—formerly minority populations
are fast becoming the collective majority. With the election
of 2008, the problem shifted quickly in character. Not only
was a Black man running for president of the United States,
but Blacks and other former minorities flocked to register to vote, and then actually voted in record numbers, and
then, in fact, elected the Black man. Barack Obama in the
Oval Office was the ultimate symbol that the White America they had fought so long and so hard to sustain—that
they, indeed, felt *entitled* to—had slipped from their grasp.
The country had at last to face its racial issues. Rather than
stepping up to the plate with both good will and a willingness to be a part of the solution, Republicans lost their
minds.

NOW, THE NEWS isn't all bad. Research—mine as well as
that of others—demonstrates that there has been, among
select groups within the population, real and significant
movement toward a more racially harmonious nation. Not
everyone lost his or her mind, certainly. Before we dive into

that news, however—and so that the news can be understood in its correct context—it's essential to provide a little understanding of the methodologies under which that research was conducted.

First, I want to discuss existing academic research on measuring racial attitudes, and, second, to explain the measure of racial antagonism that I used to analyze racial attitudes from 2008 to 2012. The two tasks are intimately related. I've drawn my measure of racial antagonism from a long history of academic research into racial attitudes, relying on the invaluable research of those who have come before me to understand American public opinion on race.

Measuring racial attitudes is a tricky business. Literature in political psychology and its existing definitions of negative racial attitudes are not without controversy. What I aim to show is that I've attempted to anticipate and address theoretical and methodological criticisms of our definition and measure by taking these controversies into account and adjusting our ideas and interpretations appropriately.

A delicate fundamental issue is how to define and discuss racial attitudes in America. Since the interest of this book is to talk about negative versus positive racial attitudes based on the white/black nexus, and how these attitudes have changed during the two campaigns and administrations of America's first African-American president, I am leaving out a significant area of research and understanding on what could typically be considered "racial attitudes." For example, I haven't analyzed Latinos' attitudes towards Blacks and their responses to Obama—that topic easily deserves a full book of its own. Rather, I've set what I view as a reasonable goal for one book: understanding whites' affective attitudes about Blacks in light of the campaign, election, and presidency of Barack Obama, so when I write of "racial attitudes" these are the attitudes to which I'm referring.

The next hurdle was knowing that, in discussing sensitive attitudes, it is easy to use terms that upset or alienate people. The most obvious and relevant example of this is the word "racism" itself, an emotionally and politically loaded word in American discourse. I've used the word freely in the narrative of this book because the frank conversation we're having requires it—but in a research setting, it can be a trigger. It is also, however, the term around which most academic arguments take place. Much existing research aims to uncover what racism currently means in America. For example, there is only moderate consensus over whether what some researchers currently define as racism—"symbolic racism"—is, in fact, racism at all. I make no claims to be measuring "racism" in my work since the term itself is ill-defined and contentious, although I do, of necessity, discuss existing research on the concept. What I have measured is negative sentiment towards Blacks, predominantly in the political and policy realm. With these cautionary statements out of the way, let's turn to a rundown of the academic view of modern racial attitudes.

ARGUABLY ONE OF the foremost theories on modern racial attitudes in America is that of "symbolic racism" first put forward in the work of the psychologist David O. Sears and Donald R. Kinder, professor of political science at the University of Michigan, in the early 1970s. Since that time, multiple theories have emerged along similar lines, all falling under a heading of what is now called "modern" or "new" racism. Scholars argued in the 1970s, and still do today, that modern racism takes on a very different form than racism did in the first half of the twentieth century. Leading up to the Civil Rights Era, racism was predominantly of the "Jim Crow" or "old-fashioned" nature, a racism in which whites believed in the genetic inferiority of Blacks, thereby justifying their negative attitudes and behaviors, many of which were overt, towards them. As these beliefs waned and/or expressing negative views about African-Americans became less acceptable, racism took on a different form.

Many scholars believe modern racism is based in American social values and white Americans' perceptions that Blacks violate these values. The primary value we're talking about is that of American individualism. American individualism is the idea that anyone can be successful in America if they simply try hard enough. Variously known as the Protestant work ethic or bootstrap mentality (as in "pulling oneself up by..."), this individualistic belief has combined with an increasingly prevalent view in America that racism is no longer a hindrance for black success, and together they create a situation in which any failure, or lack of success, on the part of Blacks is attributed to their simply not trying hard enough. Once one believes that the onus lies entirely on the individual, the attempt to incorporate other reasons, such as systemic or historical ones, becomes an affront to traditional values.

There is no doubt that white Americans do feel this way. In a survey I conducted in June 2008, I found elements of these exact sentiments in setting out to measure racial antagonism. The responses I got demonstrate a prevailing view among whites that Blacks use racism as an excuse for failure (68% believe this), that Blacks have equal opportunities with whites (61% agree), and that Blacks are responsible for any failure to get ahead (55%). Again, this combination of beliefs, whether right or wrong, leads to the view that African-Americans are not pulling their weight and as a result are violating sacred American principles.

This symbolic value and its perceived violation are what define "symbolic racism." White Americans react instinctively to African-Americans and any potentially race-based policies from within the context of these symbolic negative perceptions. The result is resentment and negative affect towards Blacks as well as opposition to policies aimed to help them get ahead, such as, but certainly not limited to, affirmative action. Rather than being based in the Jim Crow ideas of Blacks' racial inferiority, which produced the same negative effect and policy preferences, symbolic racism stems from symbolic values. In addition, this new racism is covert or implicit, rather than overt, making it difficult to measure.

Symbolic racism is typically measured through a combination of questions designed to ascertain the degree of resentment towards Blacks based on the violation of the individualism value. Sears and Kinder's first model included

measures of the respondents' beliefs on whether government paid more attention to Blacks than whites; whether
Blacks receiving welfare could actually get along without it;
whether Blacks were getting more than they were entitled
to; and whether Blacks should "push themselves where not
wanted."[133] Various other aspects have been added and sub-
tracted over the years by Sears, Kinder, and other new racism researchers, but most current conceptualizations share
these four common elements:

1 WHETHER racism or prejudice is still an obstacle to
Blacks' success;

2 WHETHER OR NOT Blacks are responsible for their
own condition in America;

3 WHETHER Blacks continue to demand special
treatment;

4 WHETHER any additional benefits or aid to Blacks is
warranted.

Those individuals perceived as symbolic racists would
generally answer no, yes, yes and no to questions measuring each of these issues.

Repeated studies demonstrate that the symbolic-politics measure (in its various forms) explains attitudes on racial policy[134] as well as whites' negative sentiments towards
Blacks generally. Others have found that the symbolic-rac-
ist attitudes (designed from the four elements above) even

include elements of old-fashioned racism.[135] In general, the sum total of research demonstrates that the symbolic-politics measure, whatever its strengths or weaknesses, does a reasonably good job capturing different but related elements of anti-Black attitudes in America today.

Despite its persistence—some might even say dominance—over the past thirty years, symbolic-politics theory has its critics. Perhaps the strongest critique comes from Paul Sniderman and his colleagues who argue that aspects of symbolic racism—namely its partial measurement through questions about individualistic values—are actually aspects of conservative principle, rather than any sort of racism or antagonism, and as such do not represent "racist" views at all, whether symbolic or not.[136] In other words, symbolic-racism measures conflate ideology and racism, and as a result, conservatives may be labeled racists by merely answering questions in a principled, ideological manner. Sniderman and his colleagues demonstrate in their experimental work that self-identified conservatives are less racist than liberals when racism is measured through hypothetical behavior, rather than individualistic, symbolic attitudes.

These two aspects of symbolic, or new, racism—that principle drives, or at least captures, racial resentment, but that conservatives' principled stands could falsely identify them as racists—also drive my measure of negative racial attitudes. While the result is in no way a perfect measure, given that four decades of research has yet to find one, it is nevertheless a reasonable measure to capture negative racial attitudes in the age of Obama.

Fig. 4.   Racial Index Component Statements and Most
          Frequent Answers

Question statement	Most frequent answer
Reverse discrimination, where whites are put at a disadvantage in order to benefit minorities, is a growing problem today.	Agree somewhat
Blacks and other minorities who can't get ahead in this country are mostly responsible for their own condition.	Agree somewhat
Often people like me feel like we are losing out or being disadvantaged because of racial preferences like Affirmative Action.	Disagree strongly
Too often minorities use racism as an excuse for their own failures.	Agree strongly
As the result of racial preferences, less qualified minorities too often get hired and promoted.	Agree somewhat
The government has gone too far in helping minorities to the disadvantage of other groups.	Disagree somewhat
It is unfair for us to have to sacrifice and pay the price, through government funded programs, today for discrimination that happened decades ago.	Agree strongly
African Americans have just as many opportunities as white people these days.	Agree strongly
The government has done enough to eliminate racial discrimination.	Agree somewhat

The central measure I used in conducting research for this book is a scale of racial antagonism. The scale is patterned on typical scales of symbolic racism[137] or racial resentment[138] that have stood the test of time and academic scrutiny. It is designed to measure the extent to which an individual feels antagonistic towards Blacks and consists of nine individual survey items, listed in *Fig. 4.* Respondents were asked the extent—"strongly" or "somewhat"—to which they either agreed or disagreed with each statement. The second column in the chart demonstrates the variance among answers to these questions by presenting the modal category for each across all four surveys. Cronbach's alpha which, in statistics, is a classical test theory for the lower estimate of reliability for a test that is psychometric in nature, for my index is .84, well above typical reliability floors—and above the typical "racial resentment" index from the ANES, which scores a .73.

One common criticism of this kind of measure, as we've already touched upon, is that it invariably captures non-racially-based attitudes of individualism, labeling them as racial animus when they are actually general policy principles. Individuals who believe in the ethos that Americans need to pull themselves up by their bootstraps and not take handouts—individualism—oppose policies aimed at helping those they feel do not help themselves. As a result, their ideological opposition to programs like affirmative action may be reflected in a racial-attitudes measure as antagonism when it could be, instead, a principled policy opposition.[139]

Another problem with ideology and symbolic racism is the possibility that principled liberal positions may serve to *hide* racial resentment. While discussed far less frequently, this possibility exists. Liberals whose ideological principles may cause them to generally defend preferential treatment and programs for the less fortunate, but who harbor negative racial attitudes, may seem *less* biased when the antagonism measure consists of individualistic principles. As a result, controlling for ideology is important to tease out the effects of racial antagonism on both ends of the ideological spectrum.

The problem then becomes how to develop a reliable measure of negative racial sentiment that neither conflates nor disguises ideological policy positions with racially-motivated attitudes and positions. Without any control for ideology we risk overstating the effects of racial attitudes for conservatives while understating them for liberals and misrepresenting some positions. On the other hand, if we control too much for ideology we will assuredly understate the effects of racial attitudes among conservatives, eliminating some attitudes that are actually racially-based under the guise of ideology. At the same time, we will overstate the potentially antagonistic views of liberals by removing ideological principle, a potentially driving force in racial opinion. Ideally we would be able to remove only the principled-policy effects from the racial-attitudes measure, but we cannot do so without repeated measures of specific policy preferences, which we do not have. As a result, I've chosen what I view to be the lesser of two evils—removing all ideological confluence.

Statistically this means I've regressed the original resentment index on ideology, and used the residual values as the ideology-free index. In effect this removes from our index all of the joint effects of ideology and racial resentment, leaving an independent racial measure. I then re-centered this measure so that the mid-point of the residuals was again equal to zero, retaining the dividing line for pro-racial and anti-racial sentiments and allowing me

Fig. 5.   Distribution of the Racial-Antagonism Index

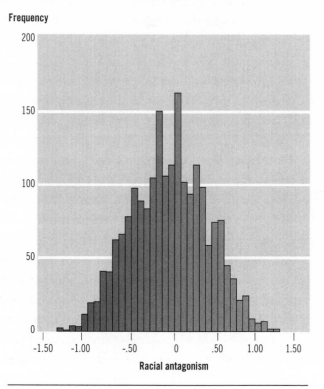

Frequency

Racial antagonism

to create a categorical measure of racial antagonism. The resulting scale ranges from -1.24 to +1.24 with higher values indicating higher levels of racial antagonism. *Fig. 5* presents the distribution of index values over all surveys among whites in the battleground states. The categorical measure consists of four groups: very positive racial views, somewhat positive racial views, somewhat negative racial views and very negative racial views. The "somewhat" categories are those individuals falling within one standard deviation of their respective side of zero (on the re-centered measure) while the "very" categories are respondents whose scores are further than one standard deviation away from 0.

I've chosen to eliminate the effects of ideology from my measure of racial resentment for multiple reasons. The first and most obvious is to avoid misstating the effects of racial attitudes in American public opinion. I find this to be a much greater sin than overstating the effects of ideology on racially antagonistic attitudes. The second and related reason is to assure readers that in this I have no ideological agenda. The goal is to dissect American opinion on race fairly—and this means giving both liberal and conservative opinions the benefit of the doubt that if their positions on a racial scale overlap with their ideology, then those positions are based on principle rather than racial affect. In other words, I believe this method of removing any doubt about the misrepresentation of ideological opinions provides the most stringent possible test of my hypotheses.

While removing the effects of ideology from the measure I also chose to remove one other problematic effect—interviewer race. Extensive research demonstrates that respondents exhibit more positive racial attitudes when being interviewed by a Black interviewer than when being interviewed by a white interviewer. Because of this, I included a dichotomous variable for having a Black interviewer in the ideological regression. As a result, the residual index is also free of interviewer race effects.

While the repeated research discussed above demonstrates that this type of symbolic-racial index captures negative racial sentiments but not sentiments more broadly—such as partisan or general policy preferences—I chose to demonstrate that again here for this particular measure. Specifically, to provide evidence of the validity of the measure as a gauge of racial attitudes we look at white individuals' views of both issues and political figures. The results demonstrate that our racial-antagonism index has a significant impact on individuals' views of Black political figures and groups but not white, and on political concerns related to race but not those unrelated.

In the initial survey I conducted in July 2008, I asked a series of questions about how worried voters were about specific issues. These included their family's financial situation, that someone in their family was going to lose their job, that they might lose a promotion at work due to "affirmative action or other racial preferences," that they or a child of theirs might not get into college because of racial preferences, and, finally, that they or a loved one would be a victim of a robbery or violent crime. The questions were designed not only to tap very salient national worries—finances and jobs—but also to measure explicitly racial policy worries—racial preferences in jobs and college admission—and finally, the implicitly racial issue of crime.

If my racial antagonism measure is, as designed, a measure of negative racial attitudes, then it should be significantly related to racial concerns, but not to non-racial concerns. In this case, I expected that the measure would have no relationship to worries about finances and job loss. In other words, an individual's positive or negative racial attitudes should not impact how much they worry about their family's financial situation or about losing their job. If, however, the measure is conflated with general policy attitudes or principles, meaning I failed to remove such effects with the ideological controls, then it could demonstrate a relationship. In contrast, the measure should be related to fears about issues that directly involve race, such as racial preferences. While racial attitudes may not influence one's worry about their job in general, once racial preferences or affirmative action are mentioned I expect racial attitudes to help explain the extent of that worry.

The final issue of crime may be a less obvious measure of racial association. Research has shown, however, a seemingly endless array of links between whites' racial attitudes and their perceptions of race and crime. For example,

Fig. 6. Effects of Racial Attitudes on Worries About Racial and Non-Racial Issues

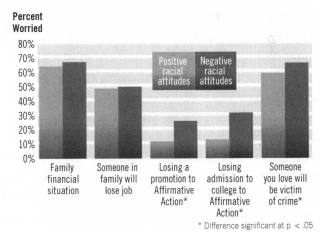

whites with negative racial attitudes are more likely to associate African-Americans with criminal behavior than they
are to associate whites with criminal behavior.[140] Whites
with negative racial attitudes are also more likely to worry
about criminal victimization by Blacks.[141] For these and
many other reasons, crime has become, in white America
at least, a racialized issue.

Fig. 6 presents a comparison of voters' concerns on these
issues between those who hold positive racial attitudes and
those with negative racial attitudes. The results confirm
that the racial-antagonism index is indeed a measure of
broad racial attitudes when it comes to issues. As expected,
racial attitudes, as measured by the index, have no impact
on white voters' strictly economic concerns: finances and
jobs. On both concerns voters with positive racial attitudes
and voters with negative attitudes have equal levels of worry.

On racial issues (both explicit and implicit), however,
our racial-antagonism index is significantly related to voters' levels of concern. Only 11% of voters with positive racial
attitudes are very worried about losing a promotion because of racial preferences, compared to 25% of voters with
negative racial attitudes. Racial attitudes explain a 14-point
gap in concern over racial promotion preferences.

Similarly, while few voters are worried about racial preferences in college admissions, there is nevertheless a 19-
point gap between voters with differing racial attitudes,
again demonstrating the heightened concern over racial issues among those with higher levels of racial antagonism.
Finally, when it comes to worrying about crime, the results
are similarly supportive of the index's validity as a measure

of racial attitudes: 66% of voters with negative racial attitudes are very worried about themselves or a loved one being a victim of violent crime, compared to 59% of those with positive racial attitudes. This is perhaps the strongest measure because the association is implicit, and not policy related.

A further step in validating the racial antagonism measure is to test its effects on voters' opinions of Black and white public figures. If the measure does correctly gauge antagonism towards Blacks, then it should have a significant impact on individuals' ratings of Black public figures but not of white public figures. Individuals with negative racial attitudes should have more negative views of Black figures than individuals with positive racial attitudes. In contrast, the two groups should demonstrate little or no difference in their ratings of white figures. This distinction is key, as the index is designed to measure sentiments regarding Blacks, not those regarding whites.

The July survey contained questions asking voters their opinions—favorable or unfavorable—about a host of public figures. Black figures included were: Barack Obama, Michelle Obama, Jesse Jackson and the NAACP (National Association for the Advancement of Colored People). White figures tested were John McCain, George W. Bush, Hillary Clinton, Joe Lieberman and Mike Huckabee. This pool provides a mix of candidates, activists, officeholders, parties and race. The one thing it lacks is a prominent Black Republican; because the purpose of the test is the Black/White difference in effects, this should not pose a problem. If white Republicans and Democrats are treated

Fig. 7.   Effects of Racial Attitudes on Opinions of White and
Black Political Actors

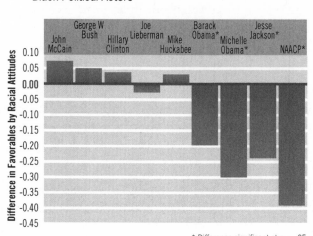

* Difference significant at p < .05

similarly, and in turn treated distinctly from Black Democratic figures, we can be confident in the index's validity as
a measure of anti-Black attitudes.

Fig. 7 contains the results of this comparison. Each bar
represents the figure's favorable rating among those with racially antagonistic attitudes minus their rating among those
with positive racial views. As a result, negative scores indicate a more negative rating from the racially negative group
while a positive score indicates a more positive one from
that group, relative to racially positive voters. In other words,
totals near zero are those with no racial effect, while those
straying either positively or negatively from zero indicate either a positive or negative net racial effect, respectively.

As expected, ratings of the Black figures—the Obamas
and Jesse Jackson and the NAACP—are substantially

more negative (statistically significantly so as well) than positive. This indicates more negative ratings among voters with racially antagonistic views than those with racially positive views. In contrast, and also as expected, both white Democrats and white Republicans show *no* difference in ratings based on racial antagonism. Huckabee, Lieberman and Clinton all receive equally favorable/ unfavorable views among racially negative voters and racially positive voters. The largest difference is only 6 points, for McCain, a negligible gap, both substantively and significantly. Overall it appears that attitudes towards Black public figures are predicted, at least in part, by racial antagonism, while views of white politicians are not.[142] This supports the use of the index as a measure of attitudes towards Blacks specifically.

These analyses of racial antagonism and issues, and racial antagonism and views of public figures demonstrate that the racial-antagonism index I use throughout this book is, in fact, a measure of racial—specifically anti-Black—attitudes, and little more. Removing the effects of voter ideology and interviewer race has left us with exactly the measure desired. We can now turn to our analysis of Americans' racial attitudes over the course of the Obama candidacy and presidency confident in the validity, both statistically and substantively, of our key measure.

So, NOW TO the news—the good and the bad. My research shows that during the month of November 2008, in the heady days following Obama's first electoral win,

Fig. 8.   Racial Aversion Over Time

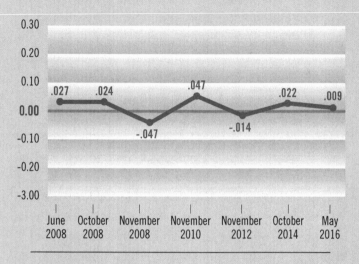

Aversion remained relatively stable going into the 2008 election, but in a moment of general historical euphoria for what had been accomplished there was a significant drop in aversion just after the '08 election, and talk of a post-racial America pulsed here in the states as well as abroad. Obama's 2008 election overall had a positive racial effect. It was, however, short-lived as governing and politics began. Republicans seized on racial terms to define Obama and his presidency, the "othering" of Obama was in full swing. Going into the 2010 mid-terms, racial aversion spiked as cries of "take back our country" rallied the Tea Party. But again, shortly after the 2012 election, we saw a very moderate drop in aversion following the President's successful argument to the nation about his leadership and vision. His second election gave us a positive racial effect. Then once again, going into the 2014 midterms, the politically-charged environment brought aversion once more to the forefront with even Democrats using dog-whistle language (the idea of being "a Clinton Democrat" as opposed to "an Obama Democrat") in an attempt to woo white voters. Our final poll chronicling the effect of the Obama presidency on racial aversion was done in the spring of 2016, as we were well into the primary battle within each party. If we were to end the exploration here at this level, we would see a rather stable long-term picture of aversion encompassing the Obama presidency with spikes/heightened aversion occurring as a powerful political tool on the Right. But the aggregate over time doesn't tell anything close to the entire and most important elements of this story. What's happening underneath tells the truly riveting political story about the country's bifurcation.

Fig. 9.   Distribution of Racial Aversion, 2008 & 2016

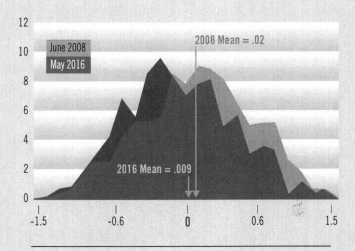

The overall average of racial aversion was slightly less (very slightly, but we'll take positives where we can get them here) in 2016 than in 2008. Aversion and the distribution of attitudes in 2008 are a little more negative.

Fig. 10. Racial Aversion by Party

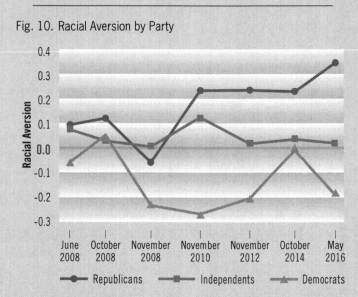

But now here is the heart of the political story. The two parties have gone in dramatically different directions over the course of Obama's presidency. In October of 2008, just before the election, all three groups (Republicans, Independents, and Democrats) were clustered around the same space, though with Republicans higher and Democrats and Independents in the same space. But what happens after the 2008 post-election euphoria is really stark and puts the surprising (to the Republican establishment) rise of Donald Trump in understandable perspective. The Black man actually entered the White House and, bam, Independents and Republicans go one way and Democrats go another on the aversion scale. While we see a real spike in aversion among Independents going into the 2010 midterm, over time they have not veered too far off the average. However, Democrats and Republicans go dramatically in different directions as over time there is volatility. Democrats grow dramatically less racial-averse from the 2008 starting point, while Republicans show just as dramatic a spike and growth in racial aversion, particularly as the primary battle is being waged.

Fig. 11. Racial Aversion by Obama and Trump Favorables

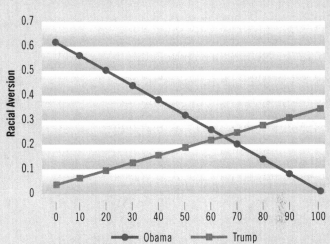

Lines chart regression estimates of the effects of each candidate's favorable
ratings on an individual's level of racial resentment.
Obama = -.006; Trump = .003.

The effects of racial aversion on Obama's favorability are very powerful—basically double the effect for Trump (.6 versus .3). Obama is
very much viewed through a racial-aversion prism—his color matters. Racial aversion affects the Black candidate dramatically but not
so much so for the white candidate; it is less relevant to the white
candidate, even when the white candidate is using racism. Racial attitudes are almost irrelevant when considering white candidates but
very strongly dictate our attitudes toward the Black man in the White
House.

there was a sharp drop in racial aversion, not just among Democrats and Independents but among Republicans as well. In fact, the decline of racial aversion among Republicans was so steep and sudden in that period that it dipped well below where the Democrats, the new president's own party, had charted just the month before, in October 2008. Overall, among Democrats, in the period from June of 2008 to May of 2016, racial aversion has dipped to an all-time low, and, among Independents, has leveled off nearly a full unit.

For Republicans, it's a whole different story. After a significantly brief honeymoon in November 2008, racial aversion among Republicans climbed precipitously, fully two and a half units in just two years, and stayed at that level until October 2014 when it again spiked—to an all-time high. Tribalism kicked in and now is running panicked and wild.

Even more illuminating in this respect is to look at the level of racial aversion as indicated by the favorable ratings of the sitting president and the 2016 Republican nominee, Donald Trump: the higher a respondent rated Obama's favorability, the lower his or her level of racial aversion; conversely, the higher a respondent rated Trump's favorability, the higher was his or her level of racial aversion. It's an inversion that couldn't be more direct, or telling. Racial aversion is, in fact, tied to Trump; yes, he is a landing place for aversion and base tribalism.

Knowing this, the reason that in just under eight years our American government has completely collapsed couldn't be clearer. A government that was formed in the heady idealism of a revolution, that survived a British invasion and the torching of the White House, and that stood even through Civil War, is today at a complete standstill. For the first time in the history of our nation, after almost eight years of race affecting every issue within the American government process, it has stopped functioning because there's a Black man in the White House—an absolute catastrophe.

> **"**If Obama was a white man, he would not be in this position....And if he was a woman (of any color) he would not be in this position. He happens to be very lucky to be who he is. And the country is caught up in the concept. **"**

Geraldine Ferraro, March 7, 2008

Before we talk about how America's racial fault lines impacted on how our first Black chief executive was able to govern, however, let's look at how it impacted his candidacy for the office. This necessarily means taking another look at some topics we've already touched upon in this book, and doing a deeper dive into those topics within the context of a presidential primary and general election race for the White House.

Former Democratic vice-presidential nominee Geraldine Ferraro's comments, above, about Barack Obama, caused a media and campaign uproar. But it was far from the only incident to put Obama's race front and center.

OF COURSE DIVING into racial conversations was not seen as productive strategy. At the heart of Obama's campaign was the theme of unity. That theme helped to play down racial divides. David Axelrod, Obama's chief strategist, told a *New York Times* reporter that his personal experience in the campaigns of Black candidates had taught him that race was not a plus when facing a diverse constituency. The *Times* detailed how the issue of race was dealt with in early meetings with campaign strategists. At one such meeting: "The race issue got all of five minutes at that meeting, setting what Mr. Obama and his advisers hoped would be the tone of a campaign they were determined not to define by the color of his skin."[143]

Perhaps as a result, the first and most serious racial firestorm in the election did not come from the campaign itself. It came from Obama's former pastor in Chicago, the Reverend Jeremiah Wright, Jr. Reverend Wright had been a powerful influence in Obama's life. According to Obama's book, *The Audacity of Hope*, Wright was responsible for Obama embracing Christianity. As the family's pastor and friend, Wright also officiated Obama's wedding, and he baptized the Obama daughters Sasha and Malia, as well as Barack himself.

In March, multiple television outlets began broadcasting past video clips of Wright's sermons from the pulpit of the Trinity United Church of Christ. The clips were troubling to say the least. Wright's sermons were energetic and inflammatory, in both style and content. As I've already pointed out in this book, for individuals not accustomed to a traditional Afrocentric preaching style—the majority of America, including the news media—the effect was dramatic and negative.

Unfortunately for the Obama campaign, voters were paying attention and they were responding negatively. According to a Pew Research Center survey after the tapes were widely broadcast, 75% of registered voters had seen or heard something (either "a little" or "a lot") about the sermons. And among these voters, 54% said they were "personally offended" by Wright's statements. Perhaps most importantly, the incident was having an impact on voters' views of the candidate. In a CBS News/*New York Times* Poll survey later that month, 36% of registered voters said they had a less favorable view of Obama as a result of the Wright tapes.

For a campaign trying to avoid the divisive issue of race, it is hard to imagine a situation more perfectly suited to upending that goal. The campaign had no choice but to address the Wright videos. As a result, on March 18, 2008, at the National Constitution Center in Philadelphia, Pennsylvania, Obama gave a speech dedicated to the one issue the campaign most wanted to avoid. The speech covered the general topic of race in America, as well as Obama's relationship with Reverend Wright, and his repudiation of Wright's views.

While virtually forced upon him, the speech was a unique opportunity for Obama to speak openly and purposefully about race, and to potentially calm the waters. Obama and his speechwriters embraced the opportunity, designing a speech that called for the American people to come together, but that was also unapologetic and pulled no punches. The combination was, as the *Wall Street Journal* put it, "a gamble."[144]

While the speech opened with warm sentiments about the founding of our country, in only the fifth sentence of the speech Obama referred to "this nation's original sin of slavery." The plight of African-Americans in American politics and society was a central theme throughout the speech. Not only did Obama talk openly about slavery and about the way Blacks were treated in early America, but he also spoke about the legacy of slavery, and more recently, racism and discrimination. It was in this context that he put Reverend Wright and his fiery sermons—as generations of pent-up resentment against an America that had never given Blacks a fair shake. Acknowledging some legitimacy in the feelings of Reverend Wright and others from his generation, while still repudiating the message itself, was a courageous move.

> "We do not need to recite here the history of racial injustice in this country. But we do need to remind ourselves that so many of the disparities that exist in the African-American community today can be directly traced to inequalities passed on from an earlier generation that suffered under the brutal legacy of slavery and Jim Crow.

"Segregated schools were, and are, inferior schools... Legalized discrimination...meant that black families could not amass any meaningful wealth to bequeath to future generations... A lack of economic opportunity among black men, and the shame and frustration that came from not being able to provide for one's family, contributed to the erosion of black families...

"This is the reality in which Reverend Wright and other African-Americans of his generation grew up. They came of age in the late '50s and early '60s, a time when segregation was still the law of the land and opportunity was systematically constricted... Even for those blacks who did make it, questions of race, and racism, continue to define their worldview in fundamental ways. For the men and women of Reverend Wright's generation, the memories of humiliation and doubt and fear have not gone away; nor has the anger and the bitterness of those years."

It would be possible, even understandable, for one to interpret Obama's litany of government neglect and even ill-will towards Blacks as a defense of the kind of statements made by Wright. And some did. Conservative columnist and pundit Charles Krauthammer wrote: "This contextual analysis of Rev. Wright's venom, this extenuation of black hate speech as a product of white racism, is not new. It's the Jesse Jackson politics of racial grievance,

expressed in Ivy League diction and Harvard Law nu-
ance."[145] The more common reaction in the press, however,
was one of praise, if at times cautious praise, for addressing the issue at all. This sentiment was typified in a head-
line in the *New York Daily News*, in a pithy style all their
own: "Bam Shows Amazing Grace, Race Speech Was
One for the Ages."[146]

Of course, for our purposes here the most important
issue is that race became a central focus of the campaign,
whether willingly or not. As Obama acknowledged in his
speech:

> **"**This is not to say that race has not been an issue
> in the campaign. At various stages in the campaign,
> some commentators have deemed me either 'too
> black' or 'not black enough.' We saw racial tensions
> bubble to the surface during the week before the
> South Carolina primary. The press has scoured every
> exit poll for the latest evidence of racial polarization,
> not just in terms of white and black, but black and
> brown as well.
>
> **"**And yet, it has only been in the last couple of weeks
> that the discussion of race in this campaign has taken
> a particularly divisive turn. **"**

And the fact that it was Obama who brought it to the
fore with thirty-seven minutes of broadcasted focus, made

it all the more noteworthy and influential. By discussing race, Obama brought attention to his own non-whiteness. As one expert put it: "The more he has to talk about race, the blacker he becomes in the public imagination."[147] This was exactly the situation the campaign had hoped to avoid in the first place, but, frankly, I knew it to be unavoidable.

Obama's speech on race has been and will continue to be endlessly dissected. But again, the central purpose here is to look at the way in which the speech brought race into the presidential context even more, and more openly, than it had been—and the context in which it was done, as an open discussion of Black resentment and mistreatment is the most important aspect for the role of race in the campaign.

THE POTENTIAL OF white voters to view Obama negatively because of race was exacerbated by a further incident, one which was far less significant to American politics in general, but that easily haunted Obama as long as the Wright controversy did. Talking to a room full of supporters in San Francisco in April, 2008, Obama discussed potential hesitation of small town and rural voters to support him. While trying to say that it was not just about race, Obama ended up saying that it pretty much was.

The media seized on Obama describing small town Pennsylvania voters as "bitter" and saying that they "cling to guns or religion." This statement had such staying power it popped up again, repeatedly, in the 2012 election as evidence of Obama's problem connecting with these voters. While this guns and religion quote provided fuel for the fire that Obama was and is an elitist who is out of touch with the average American, other parts of his comments are telling for the issue of race and the role it was playing.

What came before, and directly after the guns and religion statement, were the following, respectively:

> "Here's how it is: In a lot of these communities in big industrial states like Ohio and Pennsylvania, people have been beaten down so long. They feel so betrayed by government that when they hear a pitch that is premised on not being cynical about government, then a part of them just doesn't buy it. And when it's delivered by— it's true that when it's delivered by a 46-year-old black man named Barack Obama, then that adds another layer of skepticism."[148]

> "...they cling to guns or religion or antipathy to people who aren't like them or anti-immigrant sentiment or anti-trade sentiment as a way to explain their frustrations."[149]

While Obama's comments were not intended for public broadcast, having been spoken at a private fundraiser, he was in effect publicly acknowledging the role that race was playing in voters' willingness to support him. As it turns out, he was right.

The legacy of the primary contests and the politics surrounding them was not merely Obama as victor, but also Obama as a Black man, and more specifically, a Black candidate for president. This is not to say that Americans would not have viewed Obama as Black absent the racially-charged events of the previous five months, but there can be no doubt that the media coverage of the candidates and the candidates' actions contributed to an environment steeped in the issue of race.

American public opinion at the conclusion of the primaries was a product of this environment. Americans' attitudes toward the election were driven, in large part, by racial considerations. Americans were open to Obama and his candidacy, and their opinions of him improved in response to his nomination victory (albeit temporarily), but the extent of any individual's openness to him was significantly determined by the individual's own racial attitudes. In other words, at the beginning of the general election season, Americans were already viewing Obama through a racial lens.

Let's take a look now at the attitudes of white residents of battleground states toward Obama, and the role racial antagonism played in those attitudes at this early date. It begins with a look at how racial attitudes affected general views of Obama, then turns to racial stereotypes in America, and whether and how these battleground voters' views were affected by stereotypical views of Blacks. Finally, let's analyze how, even so early in the contest, racial attitudes affected specific electoral attitudes, including the early horserace.

The most basic measure of a candidate's image is a personal favorability measure—whether individuals view that candidate favorably or unfavorably. While candidates' images do not have to be favorable in order to win an election, especially when their opponent also suffers from unpopularity, their general image is reflected in whether or not people like them. As a result, this measure provides a useful place to start in analyzing the extent to which the American public used racial attitudes to judge Obama.

Because of Obama's race and the racially-charged electoral environment there is every reason to believe that Americans viewed him—and still do view him—through a racial lens. Given the history and sensitivity of the issue of race in America, and the frequent salience of racial attitudes in politics generally, it is likely that Americans' positive or negative views towards race were driving their attitudes towards Obama. There is little reason to believe, on the other hand, that racial attitudes had any effect on Americans' image of McCain as a person and candidate, absent Obama. Racial attitudes should certainly come into play when voters compare the two candidates, but not automatically when judging them independently.

This was indeed the case. As *Fig.* 12 demonstrates, among white voters in the battleground states, Obama's image was significantly affected by racial attitudes, while McCain's was far less influenced. The graph shows voters' favorable ratings of each candidate by the voter racial attitudes (as always, controlling for the effects of party and ideology as discussed earlier in this chapter). Three-quarters of voters with positive racial attitudes held a favorable impression of Obama in June 2008, compared to less than 40% of voters with negative racial attitudes. Racial attitudes were responsible for a 37-point difference in

Fig. 12. Effects of Racial Attitudes on the Views of Candidates

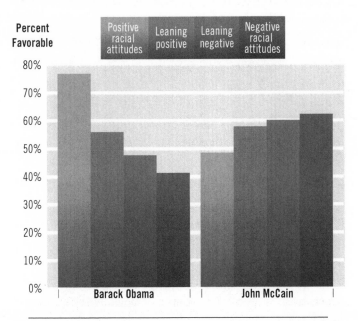

Obama's positive image. In contrast, voters' views of Mc-Cain were much less affected. Among those with positive attitudes, McCain enjoyed a 47% favorable rating, 14 points less than the 61% favorable rating he received among those with negative racial attitudes.[150]

Racial attitudes provide no explanation for battleground voters' views of McCain, but they do help to explain views of Obama, according to the June 2008 survey (and as expected by America's history of race relations). Voters were viewing Obama racially at the earliest stage of the general election race, coming out of the primaries. And this racial atmosphere was affecting his overall image. The extent of the effect does not end with a general racial division on opinions of Obama, however. Voters were also applying common racial stereotypes to him when judging him relative to McCain.

ANOTHER FACTOR DEMONSTRATING that evaluations of Obama were racial in nature at the earliest point in the general election campaign is voters' application of common racial stereotypes to him. Historically, whites have held a host of negative stereotypes of Blacks, focusing on the perceived inferiority of Blacks on multiple characteristics. For example, studies in the 1930s[151] first empirically established that negative stereotypes of Blacks in this country were that they were "lazy," "ignorant" and "stupid" among other things.[152] These stereotypes of Blacks as less industrious and less intelligent than whites persist to this day, and more recent studies have found that negative stereotypes include not only those from the 1930s, but also that African-Americans are "poor," "criminal" and "hostile."[153]

Some of these stereotypes are evident in public opinion about Obama in the June 2008 survey. Among the racial stereotypes voters applied to Obama, the most powerful was that of his having received unfair advantages in life, and not having earned what he has gotten. This was a recurring theme in the primary campaign highlighted, or perhaps even triggered, by the argument that Obama had not "paid his dues" as a politician before running for the highest office in the land, having served less than a full term as United States Senator from Illinois and having served seven years in the Illinois state senate. Politicos viewed Obama as a brash young line-jumper. Media and pundit views of Hillary Clinton were similar—the story was that she had used New York's junior U.S. Senate seat merely as a stepping stone to run for the presidency, a job for which she was not qualified.

Only one side of this story appears to have caught on with the public, however. When it came to appropriate experience, Americans viewed Obama as not measuring up, while viewing Hillary as having the right experience to run for the presidency. In response to a CNN question about whether or not each candidate had "the right experience to be president,"[154] six in ten Americans reported that Hillary Clinton had the right experience. In contrast, only 40% of Americans felt Obama had the right kind of experience, a substantial twenty-point difference.

This kind of differentiation by the public demonstrates a powerful racial stereotype in America. Because Blacks are viewed as less industrious or "lazy" by many Americans, successful Blacks are viewed with suspicion. Combined with the well-known and documented backlash from affirmative action programs, this culminates in the belief, or at least suspicion, among many whites, that successful Blacks achieve what they do only because of racial preferences. As a result, any successful African-American, man or woman, is suspect as having received advantages (through such programs) that whites do not receive in order to achieve success. As we've already noted, this belief, stemming from historical Black stereotypes, is a key component to racial resentment as well.

Fig. 13. Voters' Views of the Candidates on Stereotypical
Characteristics

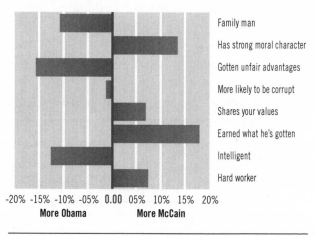

Not coincidentally, this and other traditional stereotypes were factors in battleground-states voters' views of
Barack Obama in the beginning of the general election
season. We asked voters whether or not various characteristics—designed in part to measure racial stereotypes—
better described John McCain or Barack Obama. Two of
those were measures of undeserved advantage, and voters
expressed the sentiment, on both, that Obama may have
been the beneficiary of such advantages—at least that he
was significantly more likely to have been unfairly advantaged than McCain was.

Fig. 13 contains these and other attributes and voters'
judgments of which candidate each attribute described
more. Obama was viewed as more likely to have "benefited
from unfair and undeserved advantages" than was McCain,
by nearly 15 points—30% said Obama had received unfair

advantages, compared to only 16% who said McCain had. Voters were similarly, by 16 points, more likely to believe the phrase "has earned what he has gotten in life" described McCain better than it did Obama.

This chart demonstrates some of the other common racial stereotypes at play as well. At this point in the race, McCain enjoyed the advantage on two stereotypical weaknesses of Blacks, those of being "lazy" (i.e. not hard workers) and of suspect moral character. In line with stereotypes of Blacks as "criminal", McCain was rated thirteen points more likely to have "strong moral character" than Obama. Similarly, Obama was rated as slightly more likely to be corrupt. McCain was seen as more of a hard worker by 7% of voters.

The one characteristic that clearly bucks the stereotype trend is voters' opinion of Obama as being better described by the term "intelligent" than McCain was, by a full 14 points. Traditionally whites have stereotyped Blacks as unintelligent, or even "stupid", making this finding seem like an anomaly. Recent research, however, helps to explain this finding. Susan Fiske and her colleagues have found that whites stereotype Blacks differently according to the subject's social status.[155] Specifically, people stereotype professional Blacks as significantly more "competent" than they view "poor Blacks." Obama, a lawyer by training, certainly fits this professional Black category. Additionally, a half-century of research demonstrates that people are willing to make individual exceptions to a stereotype when there is ample reason.[156]

Overall, these traits tell a stereotype story—voters

attributed to Obama, relative to McCain, many of the traditional stereotypes whites have attributed to Blacks over the years. There is, however, an alternative explanation to these numbers, which is that voters may have simply been expressing what they were seeing and hearing, and coming to believe, from the campaigns. As discussed earlier, Obama was the young, relatively inexperienced candidate. In contrast, McCain's history lent itself to the image of a fighter who had made it through very tough times, as a prisoner of war no less, to get where he was—a long-standing, experienced member of the United States Senate.

This raises an important question: how do we tell the difference between the "facts," or at least the images that have bases in reality, and stereotyping? Without a controlled experiment, it is nearly impossible. What is possible, however, is to examine whether or not these images of the candidates contain a racial dimension. Are voters' opinions about the candidates' attributes tied to voters' attitudes on race? If they are then we have strong evidence for the stereotype side of the argument. For this analysis we again use the racial-index measure that captures racial attitudes but not ideological attitudes, and we look at the trait advantages voters ascribe to the candidates, based on voters' racial attitudes.

In general, the results, as illustrated in *Fig. 14*, demonstrate that those battleground voters with more negative racial attitudes also have more negative views of Obama's personal traits than do voters with positive racial views. It is worth reemphasizing at this point that the racial-attitudes measure has been purged of ideological effects. In

Fig. 14. Effects of Racial Attitudes on Voters' Stereotypical
Views of the Candidates

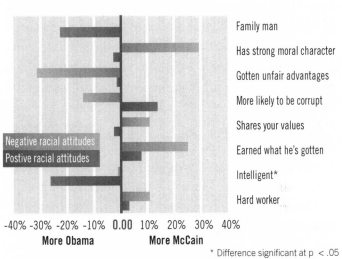

Family man

Has strong moral character

Gotten unfair advantages

More likely to be corrupt

Shares your values

Earned what he's gotten

Intelligent*

Hard worker

Negative racial attitudes
Postive racial attitudes

-40% -30% -20% -10% **0.00** 10% 20% 30% 40%
More Obama   **More McCain**

* Difference significant at p < .05

other words, these differences are not attributable to liberalism or conservatism.

The relationship between racial attitudes and views of the candidates is true not only in simple cross tabulations, but also in ordinal regression models. In a set of seven models with each trait as the dependent variable, and while controlling for individuals' party affiliation and their affective preference between the candidates (the difference in their favorable rating of Obama minus McCain), racial antagonism significantly affects four of the seven traits (see notation in the chart). This means that, by and large, racial attitudes are telling a fair share of the trait story—that of Obama as subject to stereotypical judgments. These are

not merely standard party, ideological or candidate preferences at work.

Some of the largest racial-attitude differences on candidate traits are found on the traditional racial stereotypes. Regarding which candidate is more likely to have
gotten unfair advantages in life, race-negative voters are
twenty-nine points more likely to say Obama has than
McCain has, compared to race-positive voters who are divided on which candidate is more unfairly advantaged. On
both character issues—strong moral character and corruption—there is roughly a thirty-point difference between
the two groups, with race-negative voters consistently rating Obama as the more morally questionable. Only on the
traits of sharing voters' values, being a hard worker, and
having earned what he's gotten (both race-negative and
race-positive voters favoring McCain on this measure)
there are not statistically significant differences between
the two groups, although each still works marginally in
McCain's favor.

While the numbers in this chart made it look as if voters' ratings of the candidates' bucked the stereotypic image
of African-Americans as less intelligent than whites, we
see that racial attitudes *are* actually affecting this rating.
While voters with negative racial attitudes are divided over
which candidate is better described by the term "intelligent," voters with positive racial attitudes are significantly
more likely to choose Obama on this characteristic. While
Obama is seen as more intelligent overall, there is nevertheless a significant divide, created by racial antagonism, over
the description. This is precisely what we would expect to

see if racial stereotypes were at work in shaping individuals' images of Obama.

In contrast to these stereotypical measures, traits that have little or no apparent connection with race are not affected by voters' racial attitudes, again exactly as one would expect. For example, when asked which candidate was more likely to raise their taxes, there are no significant differences between those with positive racial attitudes and those with negative racial attitudes. All agreed that Obama was the more likely to do that.

In summary then, not only do we find that the public in general views Obama through a racial stereotype prism, but also, racial opinion drives much of the effect. Again it is important to emphasize that this is true even after we've removed all affects of ideology from the racial attitudes measure, and in this case also controlled for party preferences and favorable/unfavorable judgments towards the candidates. In other words, these race-negative voters are not Republicans or conservatives, or even merely fans of John McCain whose views are driven by policy, principle, or simple candidate preferences. These are racial stereotypes and negative racial affect at work. The Presidency of Obama would be viewed first and foremost from the lens of tribalism and let's stop pretending it's primarily about something else other than his race.

IF THE ELECTORAL race was significantly impacted by race, could it be a surprise that, once Barack Obama was in office, race would remain an issue? Perhaps what we could say *was* surprising was that racial polarization as a primary problem in governing during Obama's time in office became apparent so very quickly.

Republicans opposed every single idea Obama was for, and this in spite of the fact that many of the ideas were theirs to start with. In fact, there is a term for it: *blacksliding*. Based on the verb "backslide", which means to revert to old ways or habits, *blacksliding* means to oppose a good idea one formerly supported based solely on the fact that Obama thinks it's a good idea, too. For example, Republicans once loved Merrick Garland,[157] but now that Obama has nominated him for the Supreme Court they don't like him at all and are blacksliding. It's a fine word for the eye-popping hypocrisy with which the right has met the task of governing alongside their first Black Chief Executive, funny and apt at the same time. But don't laugh too hard—what they have been doing for eight years is irrational and dangerous: starkly, and properly, the right has demonstrated time and time and time again that they'd rather sink the country and see its citizens suffer than do business with a Black man.

Let us count the ways.

1 THE TROUBLED ASSET RELIEF PROGRAM (TARP)
   is one of the measures the federal government
   undertook in 2008 to address the subprime mortgage
   crisis. It was a program to purchase toxic assets
   from financial institutions in order to shore up the
   country's financial sector and prevent its collapse,
   and it had the support of Republicans in Congress

who helped to push it through the legislature so
George W. Bush could sign it on October 3, 2008.
Republicans loved getting the credit when they
presented stimulus checks back home, to their
local constituents, and the program, under the
efficient stewardship of the Obama administration,
was accomplished far under budget—some $200
billion under budget.[158] Yet, when Obama proposed
using some of that windfall for a jobs stimulus
package, Republicans suddenly once again became
very worried about debt reduction. Think of it:
Republicans in Congress passed—and a Republican
president signed into law—a bailout bill that
served the country's financial sector, the very sector
that had caused the need for a bailout in the first
place; however, although the program had been
administered effectively, and far less expensively
than imagined, by the Black Democrat in the
Oval Office, Republicans opposed the president's
measures to create jobs for the middle class, the very
people whose taxes had just bailed out the financial
sector. One can more than fairly suggest that the
concern the Republicans shared was far less about
debt reduction and far more about a Black president
being further legitimized by efficiently administering
another successful program—really, how would it
look if President Obama, and the liberal policies he
was capably stewarding, was able to so commendably
resolve the then-current nationwide jobs crisis?
Republicans, in other words, could more easily live

with the unemployment rate remaining high than they could with Obama administering yet another successful economic recovery program.

2 WHILE WE'RE ON THE SUBJECT OF DEFICIT SPENDING, it isn't a secret that Republicans have been, from time to time, all for it. Under Ronald Reagan, the national debt doubled, and it doubled again under George W. Bush. Under Democratic presidents, however, deficit spending becomes a nonstarter to Republicans in Congress. This issue came to an ugly head during Obama's administration, over the *debt ceiling*. The debt ceiling is the upper limit on the amount of money our government can borrow to conduct its business. Importantly, it is the upper limit on the amount of money the government can borrow to fulfill obligations *it has already incurred*. Increasing the debt ceiling had always been an exercise that was conducted in a bipartisan way, as routine business, because it was, and remains, an act that simply pays for expenditures Congress had already authorized. In 2011, however, the bickering in Congress and "political brinksmanship"[159] displayed during what became an unprecedented debt ceiling debate, by the wave of anti-Obama, Tea Party loyalists that swept into the legislature in 2010, led Standard & Poor's to downgrade the United States' credit rating *for the first time in the country's history*. Republicans created the debt ceiling crisis out of whole cloth, and accepting the degradation of the country's credit rating was, for them, a fair trade-off for the satisfaction of throwing another stumbling block in the way of the Obama administration. Fortunately—and rightly— voters held the Tea Party/Republicans responsible for the historic humiliation, giving them a full 72% disapproval rating for the way they handled negotiations.[160]

3 ON THE SUBJECT OF NUKES: "A nuclear war cannot be won and must never be fought. The only value in our two nations possessing nuclear weapons is to make sure they will never be used. But then would it not be better to do away with them entirely?" So asked Ronald Reagan in his 1984 State of the Union address. In 2015, forty-seven Republican Senators stepped all over Ronald Reagan's goal by attempting to interfere with President Obama's negotiation of a nuclear deal with Iran. They sent an "open letter," addressed to "leaders of the Islamic Republic of Iran" with the intent to unravel a framework for a nuclear agreement that was already drawing to a successful close.[161] This was an unprecedented event: U.S. lawmakers seeking to undermine a U.S. president's foreign policy by appealing directly to a foreign power. And it came on the heels of another unprecedented event: then-Speaker of the House John Boehner providing the leader of a foreign power, Prime Minister Benjamin Netanyahu, a platform to speak against the same deal at a joint meeting of Congress. U.S. legislators trying to make an

end-run around a sitting president by appealing to
foreign powers had, simply, never before happened in
American history. It showed the depth of the disdain
and disrespect these Republicans had for President
Obama. And placing the interests of another country
ahead of their obligations to the United States? Well,
that came as close to the water's edge of treason as
any members of any Congress before it had ever
dared.

I could go on. From healthcare mandates (an idea
hatched by conservative economists[162]) to infrastructure
spending (Republican administrations had brought us our
transcontinental railways and the Interstate Highway System[163]), from gutting civil rights protections (a Republi-
can-majority Supreme Court had ruled in Brown v. Board
of Education), to gutting environmental protections (over
a hundred years later the word "conservationist" resonates
as a defining description of Republican President Theodore Roosevelt), there really is no shortage of examples
that demonstrate just how thoroughly Republicans have
flip-flopped on their own core values over the decades, or
how intensely the normal and even healthy partisan opposition ramped up once Barack Obama had taken office.

The frustration that progressives feel for the intensity
and intransigence of this opposition can be summed up in
a little gallows humor: if President Obama found a cure for
cancer, Republicans would attack him for trying to put the
drug industry out of business.

On the other side of the aisle, you're apt to hear Republicans disingenuously defending their actions by insisting they are merely acting as the Loyal Opposition. Indeed, this was the rationalization Mitch McConnell offered up when he was asked to explain exactly what he meant when he said, during Obama's first term, that his number one priority was to make Obama a one-term president.[164] Others, like Rush Limbaugh, delivered the same message, if with less subtlety—"I hope he fails!"—but their justifications for wishing failure on an American presidency were the same: "...what is unfair about my saying I hope liberalism fails?"[165] While it's usually difficult to prove causation, the evidence here is overwhelming: the Right does not accept the validity of a Black man as president *because he is Black*—and, because they couldn't legitimately defeat him in two elections, they are going to discredit him. Failing that, they are going to do things like prevent a jobs program that could bring relief to hundreds of thousands of struggling middle-class families, they're going to smear the sterling credit of the country they supposedly love, and they're going to try to sink international nuclear arms deals. They're going to take their country back, or they're going to take it down.

This all only makes sense through the prism of tribal angst and racial polarization. You see, a Black man in the White House is a cataclysmic event, and thus all the normal historic rules of the road go out the door. There's a Black man in the White House, nothing else but destroying that matters. It is why the "party of Lincoln," a party that is indeed old, and that once was grand, deteriorated into a party that, circa 2016, can put up a flat-out racial

antagonist like Donald J. Trump as their party's nominee for president. A person who the vast majority—60%
according to a *Washington Post* poll[166]—of voters understands holds bias against women and minorities is now the
standard-bearer for the Republican Party in 2016. Not 1916,
but 2016.

We've come a long way.

AS LONG AS there have been American politics, racism
has been a part of them, whether covert like the dog whistle of the Southern Strategy, or overt like the rantings of
George Wallace.[167] George Wallace, however, let us be clear,
was never the presidential nominee of a major party. But
because of the catastrophe of a Black man in the White
House his modern reincarnation is not only the nominee
but is, depending on which poll you look at as of this writing, either tied or just a couple of points down in the contest to be president.

There's no doubt, when sorting racists by type, that
Donald J. Trump falls into the overt category. He's a notorious birther who thinks Mexicans are rapists and all Muslims should be banned from entering the United States;
case closed. That Trump went further, both in his willingness to make egregious and blatant racist statements
and through the political process, than anyone could have
reasonably predicted, shouldn't actually be a real surprise—America is in crisis mode, and it is during crises
that guys like Trump rise. The crisis this time is racial polarization, as our data shows; while other crises from war

to natural disasters have brought our country closer together, this is the one that now threatens to tear us apart because it is the unique disaster that sends us in opposite corners. It is the unique disaster that is the sum of all our country's fears dating back to the time that an African landed in chains on these shores—the upending of white political rule.

Barack Obama symbolizes a new country. Former minorities are not yet the collective majority, but *a* minority is now head of the government, and that's the key driver in the heightened racial aversion we're now experiencing in America. Fifty years ago, George Wallace couldn't have risen to become the nominee of a major American political party because the wolf of diversity and demographic change wasn't at the door. But when Barack Obama was elected, suddenly the wolf was real. The need to take back their country from the brown and Black people who were usurping it—the need to assert continued white superiority and supremacy—became urgent. We shouldn't be surprised that in a highly racially charged environment, a blustering strong man would rise to fill the vacuum. Trump's base has found, in his candidacy, their voice: someone who will speak for those who perceive civil rights as a zero-sum game. That Barack Obama is not, as the Right suggests, to blame for worsening racial tensions in this country, doesn't mean that he hasn't been the catalyst we need to finally and openly deal with the problem of the color line that's been hanging over our heads for nearly four hundred years now.

I HASTEN TO add that Trump's base is not made up of Republican party regulars; to smear all Republicans with one broad stroke is to dismiss the honorable tenets of the party's foundation, as well as to undermine the two-party system itself which has, in the past, provided vigorous and beneficial debate that perfects the laws that emerge from our legislative chambers. But the Republican Party has come to a reckoning point—it must figure out (nod here to J.E.B Bush and the like) how to confront the no-longer-covert racialization component now at the center of its party, or watch the party be destroyed as the demographic changes taking place move it squarely out of any hope of governing. I believe it must choose the former in order for our government to continue to function, as it was designed to do, with checks and balances.

I also feel compelled to underscore that, as a country, we haven't gotten more racist over the years—or, indeed, in the last eight years—but that the demographics of our country are changing and events have come to pass that have brought out the worst of the latent racism that has been buried within the American experiment for too many centuries.

Finally, I don't want to label those people who have thrown their support behind Trump as, simply, "bad" people. I argue that we should try to understand why they feel threatened—and to take a moment to see that, from their perspective, it makes logical sense to feel threatened. As a social scientist, I observe and track trends, but as a citizen who wants our country to move forward—who wants to solve this problem—I can't stress strongly enough that in order to create solutions, you can't shut any group of people out of the discussion. You can't slam the door. You always have to bring them in, and allow yourself to walk in their shoes in order to find resolution.

So, where does this leave us? Certainly, at a crossroad. Are the Republicans going to be part of the solution, or are they going to remain the party of resentment? Will they step up now to reassert their relevance in a country of enormous and rapid demographic and social change, or will they go the way of the Whigs? How are we, as a country, going to handle the future?

The first step in solving any problem is, of course, recognizing and acknowledging that there *is* a problem. And, make no mistake about it, we have a problem. The folks who would rather torch the place than play ball if they can't get their way? They have set the house on fire.

Conclusion

> **"God showed Noah the rainbow sign,
> no more water but fire next time."** [168]

There are three components that must be present to create fire. Fuel—something that will burn; heat—something to keep the fuel burning; and oxygen.

The fuel in our fire is resentment. Often politicians and pundits will assume the resentment is based on economics. In 2016 that's surely the way it seems the argument has been framed—the Republican candidate stoking the fears of hardworking, middle-class whites that their jobs are being stolen by brown immigrants from south of the border, that affirmative action means their child's place in college is going to go to a less qualified Black kid; that their tax dollars are being used to support Middle Eastern refugees. Indeed, progressives are frequently befuddled by this phenomenon: hardworking, middle-class whites voting against their perceived own economic interests by backing candidates who support policies that are diametrically opposed to the everyday pocketbook interests of the working and middle class—but who are oh so skillful at shifting the blame for stagnant wages and slow job growth away from their own opposition to proactive economic programs and onto the backs of any "other" who happens to be on trend. The problem is, of course, as we have quantified in these pages, not one of economics but of racial aversion/ tribal polarization. Historically in America—and particularly in the American South—your class has been determined not so much by your educational level or the number of zeros on your paycheck, but by your race. In America race is your class. This is why it's almost impossible that a serious, broad-based populist economic movement of the kind we've seen in most of the industrialized west that fundamentally helps every day, working-class whites would ever take root in the United States. From fighting for a livable wage in the face of record corporate profits, to childcare, to universal healthcare—which is a right that isn't even debated any longer in most of western Europe—poor whites and poor Blacks have never been truly united in a manner which would force a populist challenge. W.E.B Dubois discussed in his book, *Black Reconstruction*, how, after the Civil War, the poor white was in many ways just as badly off as the recently freed slave, but the hungry poor whites were fed Jim Crow and they ate—they ate until they were full. Rich or poor, smart or dumb, in the South my ancestors, no matter how hard they worked, could and would never raise above the level of nigger. Sustaining this division between the races is *exactly*, of course, what the established power brokers and other millionaires and billionaires, like Trump, want—imagine the real and effective threat the working class would pose to their cultural hegemony if all the colors among it banded together! But that banding together isn't around the corner as I write today, and so, even as college-educated whites pull back from Trump, he is running up record support margins among non-college-educated whites—the working class who, instead of realizing the power they could wield if they united with their black and brown peers, feel particularly threatened by their rise.

FRAMING THE ARGUMENT around the economy blinds us to the real source of resentment, which is, of course, the "others" themselves. These hardworking, middle-class whites aren't voting *against* their economic interests, but *for* their higher interest; they are voting their values—and what they value is society as they have always known it. A country where their culture, and their skin color, is dominant. They believe they are losing their culture, but they are hanging onto their whiteness to define themselves. Take a look at the accompanying chart, in which we calculated the probability of an Obama favorability advantage based on a respondent's racial attitudes, and the driving force behind which candidate got ticked in the ballot box becomes clear.

The heat in our analogy can, in 2016, be personified as Donald Trump, a Republican Party presidential nominee who shamelessly calls brown people rapists, seriously proposes banning members of an entire religion from the country, and gleefully retweets memes garnered from white supremacist web sites. But as I hope I've made obvious in the pages of this book, Donald Trump isn't an original threat; he's only the culmination of decades of racial antagonism by a Republican Party that has depended for so long on its Southern Strategy and other such power tools to keep the loyalty of an increasingly white base that their cynicism has finally caught up with them. The chickens have indeed come home to roost.

And our oxygen? Some say it's a media that has coddled the 2016 Republican front runner.[169] That has refused for over an entire year to use the word 'lie'[170] about the things that come out of his mouth, even though that's the correct term for, as Politifact indicates, a minimum of 70% of what he says.[171] That has, in some particularly cringe-worthy episodes, gone so far as to try to make him seem harmless, and cuddly.[172] Sure, OK, and yeah, I suppose—the media has been a breeze that fanned the flame. But blaming the media for the continuing misadventures of Donald J. Trump is too glib. And it's also inaccurate.

Look at the fire we're studying through this lens: Donald Trump is the embodiment of the racial-power problem, and his campaign paints a clear picture of how our power structure works. Trump's race-baiting strategy aside for a moment, ask yourself: if Donald Trump where Black could he be where he is now, one of only two people who will in fact be the next president of the United States? Could someone who makes declarations on a regular basis that are patently just not true, who ignores basic norms regarding transparency (he continues to ignore calls from both parties, including the Republican Party's 2012 nominee Mitt Romney, to release his taxes like every presidential nominee in modern history has done), who 60% of voters think isn't qualified to be president, who a majority believe doesn't have the temperament to be president—could a Black person with this resumé come within striking distance of the office of president? Of course not. But Trump doesn't have to tell the truth, he doesn't have to have a real grasp of the complex issues, he doesn't have to have the temperament to be president, all he has to be is the Great White Hope, the great tribal warrior, to garner a majority of white support and run up advantages among non-college whites, and that's enough to keep him within striking distance of the nuclear codes. And this is why we must wage a battle against racism—as the country continues to change demographically, continued racial animosity undermines our ability as a country to win the future. It puts all that generations of Americans have worked and fought to create in peril. The gust of wind that makes the whole fire roar is, again, a matter of race, the wolf at the door, the country's changing demographics, the catastrophe of a Black man in the White House which brings it all home and into complete focus. As I've said before, the Dixiecrat George Wallace could not have been a major party presidential nominee when he ran in 1968 because, while his extreme politics might have appealed to a certain segment, there was at the time no clear and present danger to his natural constituency that the white majority was losing its dominant status. The contemporary, rapidly changing nature of the United States' population is what has made our politics so combustible.

The questions now become: Is it possible to put out the fire? Is it possible to douse it before it destroys what too many poor Blacks and poor whites have sweated, bleed, fought, and died to build—the strongest, most powerful, most prosperous nation the world has ever known. Is there a firebreak we can employ to stop the damage?

In 2004, John Kerry got the same percentage of the white vote that Barack Obama got in 2008—43%. John Kerry lost by three million votes. The difference between Kerry's losing coalition and Obama's winning one? The dramatic difference in the number of minority votes, in particular Black votes: 11.8 million Black voters cast their ballots for Kerry; four years later, 15.5 million cast their ballots for Obama. Turning out the Black vote, and making sure that Blacks who show up at the polls actually get to vote,[173] are, as everyone on each team in the 2016 contest knows, essential in keeping Donald Trump from emblazoning his brand name on the nation's White House. In 2016 *Black votes matter*. They are, make no mistake, critical in assuring that, come January 2017, the United States does not have a blatant racist sitting in the Oval Office. You can't miss the irony here: given that Trump is currently running well ahead of Clinton among white voters, and will win white voters comfortably, the only thing standing in the way of this objectively unqualified man becoming the next U.S. president will be the political power wielded at the ballot box by the growing minority voters—who are, in fact, the predicate for his rise in the first place.

But as crucial as the enthusiasm of Black voters is on Election Day 2016, and even assuming that we get the job done and prevent the real catastrophe of a Trump presidency, a victory in November 2016 is, in truth, only a firewall against the real blaze we'll have to continue to fight and control long after this election is history. And the first step we'll have to take in the long fight is to decide to stop pretending we are not a racially polarized nation.

Admitting that we have a problem, and accepting the scope of it, is the only way to get past the current incendiary tribalization that is deteriorating our ability to function as a nation. If we are to have any hope of retaining our status as the world's great nation, we must bridge the gaps between ourselves and "others."

Part of the solution will have to be a willingness, on both sides, to move beyond stereotypes. That is, fear of a changing cultural makeup—and the accompanying necessity of readjusting one's comfort zone—does not automatically make one a bad person. Progressives have to allow that, as society is rapidly changing around us, the world of fear is not an entirely irrational place to land.

It is, however, a wholly unreasonable place to want to *live*. But what will save us from this uninhabitable place? A focused commitment to education, to the nurturing of the understanding that equality among the races, as our society defines that term, is not a zero-sum game. You don't have to lose in order for me to win. This is a key component of the work ahead, but it isn't *the* key.

Repentance is.

The Biblical concept of repentance is to turn from evil, toward the good. Our nation turned from the evil of slavery about a hundred and fifty years ago—but, to this day, we have, as a nation, never defined for ourselves what the good we are turning *toward* is supposed to be. Let me put this in the context of another nation that has lately turned away from evil.

Nazi Germany was responsible for some of the most horrific war crimes ever committed by an empire. Six million Jews were systematically murdered, or died from abuse in concentration camps under the regime. Deaths among members of the armed forces, and deaths of civilians either through military actions or due to war-related famine and disease bring the total body count for World War II to somewhere between fifty and eighty million. After her defeat, and in addition to paying reparations to nations around the world too numerous to list here, the German people performed two other remarkable acts that demonstrated their understanding of how deeply the country's actions had damaged nations and peoples around the globe. First, the country made it illegal for her citizens to belong to neo-Nazi organizations, and banned ownership of Nazi paraphernalia, excepting only those items that were retained for their historical significance, such as items owned by a museum; to this day you cannot legally display a swastika on German soil. Second, Germany has apologized for its part in the world's bloodiest war—and it continues, over seventy years later, to offer its contrition, most recently in May of 2015 when Chancellor Angela Merkel made the trip to Moscow "to commemorate the end of the war in Europe and gave a statement that said Nazi Germany was 'responsible' for millions of dead during the conflict."[174] Though few Germans who participated in WWII are still alive today, the steps that the country took to demonstrate not only remorse for the evil actions perpetrated in its name, but also the determination to become and remain an honorable nation once again, has earned it continued respect around the globe.

In contrast, the American South has never apologized

for waging a civil war against her own countrymen. America has never formally expressed remorse for holding over four million Blacks in slavery for over four hundred years. And the paraphernalia of the regime that held these four million people in chains? It is only recently that the Confederate flag has been removed from state houses in the American South; displaying this symbol of the worst America has ever had to endure—this emblem of oppression, and pain, and bondage, and death—is still legal in the country that suffered under it.

The Bible tells us, "Repent ye therefore, and be converted, that your sins may be blotted out, when the times of refreshing shall come from the presence of the Lord."[175]

America—not Americans as individuals, but America as a society—has yet to repent for the gravest sins in her history. We have yet to be refreshed through confession of our greatest failings. An apology cannot be accepted if it isn't offered; healing can't truly begin until repentance is made.

> **"I tell you, Nay: but, except yet repent, ye shall all likewise perish."**[176]

As Americans, we have to start looking at what I call the Big We. Throughout most of our country's history, we've been motivated by the "small we"—ourselves, our families, our immediate tribes. But, as surely as the discovery of the New World rocked the conventions and expanded the possibilities for the people of the early-16th century, our contemporary, evermore globalized marketplace requires that we shake off conventions that no longer serve us, and expand our concept of ourselves as a nation. If we don't, then, flatly, we will not be able to compete within that marketplace and we will lose the future.

Within the next two decades, the United States will reach a demographic tipping point. The approach of this tipping point is already challenging our nation in ways that are proving hard for some folks to cope. The fire that was ignited during the presidential election of 2016 may very well burn dangerously for a long time after the election is over, no matter its outcome. And we may never craft a completely "post-racial" society for ourselves, but, moving forward, we can either strive to create a racially harmonious one in which we rise as a whole people, becoming the Big We—or we can hold on to white power and all fail together. As long as I continue to be a nigger, and the Hispanics and Muslims continue to be seen as the dangerous threatening hoards at the gate, we cannot win the future. The moment, however, that we all become simply fellow Americans striving for a better life, that's when we can be certain the sun will never set on this grand experiment in Democracy.

Acknowledgments

Shout out to Professor Monika McDermott, without whom this data-laced rant wouldn't be possible; my partner in data exploration, teacher, and, most importantly, drinking buddy.

About the Author

CORNELL BELCHER is an award-winning pollster and one of the premier strategists in national progressive politics. His polling was the blueprint for the heralded 50-State Strategy as Pollster for the Democratic National Committee (DNC) under Chairman Howard Dean—Cornell was the first minority to be lead pollster for either national party. He also served on the polling team for both Obama presidential campaigns, and has worked with both Senate and House Democrats as Senior Political Advisor to the Democratic Senatorial Campaign Committee (DSCC), Special Projects Director for the Democratic Congressional Campaign Committee (DCCC), and Women VOTE! Coordinator for EMILY's List. In 2015 he was an Institute of Politics (IOP) Fellow at Harvard University's Kennedy School. He is a highly sought after political commentator, and is currently President of brilliant corners Research & Strategies, *www.brilliant-corners.com*.

Uptown Professional Press is an imprint of Water Street Press, in partnership with Uptown Ventures Group, publishing books that focus on diversity issues and progressive politics. Look for other titles, including *101 Ways to Enjoy the Mosaic: How to Create a More Diverse Community in Your Own Backyard* by Skot Welch, *A Ghost of Sarah Palin* by Anonymous, and *Glory: A Life Among Legends*, a memoir by Dr. Glory Van Scott—all coming soon.

www.waterstreetpressbooks.com

Notes

1. http://fortune.com/2016/06/17/california-france-6th-largest-economy/

2. http://www.whitehousehistory.org/history/white-house-timelines/african-americans-1900s-1940s.html.

3. http://www.history.com/news/history-lists/8-things-you-might-not-know-about-booker-t-washington/print.

4. http://downwithtillman.com.

5. *Manliness and Civilization: A Cultural History of Gender and Race in the United States, 1880–1917*, Gail Bederman, University of Chicago Press, 2008.

6. http://www.nytimes.com/2016/03/31/us/politics/donald-trump-abortion.html?_r=0.

7. https://www.washingtonpost.com/politics/trump-pushes-expanded-ban-on-muslims-and-other-foreigners/2016/06/13/c9988e96-317d-11e6-8ff7-7b6c1998b7a0_story.html.

8. http://www.theatlantic.com/politics/archive/2016/06/trump-mexican-judge/485429/.

9. http://www.vanityfair.com/news/2016/06/donald-trump-tv-network.

10. Ibid.

11. https://www.youtube.com/watch?v=hpPt7xGx4Xo.

12. See Ronald Reagan's speech in support of Barry Goldwater at the 1964 Republican convention.

13. http://www.splcenter.org/blog/2009/11/24/anti-black-hate-crimes-rise-data-remains-flawed/.

14. http://www.civilrights.org/publications/hatecrimes /african-americans.html.

15. http://www.nbcnews.com/id/27799810/ns/us_news -life/t/mayor-sorry-kids-assassinate-obama-chant /#.VYaWeM673S4.

16. http://www.masslive.com/news/index.ssf/2008/11 /suspicious_blaze_destroys_tink.html?category =Springfield.

17. Excerpted from "The Examination of Benjamin Franklin," 1766, published in *The Parliamentary History of England from the Earliest Period to the Year 1803*, 1813.

18. http://www.huffingtonpost.com/2012/11/16 /secession-poll_n_2147048.html.

19. http://www.huffingtonpost.com/brendan-demelle/study -confirms-tea-party-_b_2663125.html.

20. http://www.post-gazette.com/opinion/2008/11/06 /america-wins-obama-s-election-is-a-historic-pivotal -moment/200811060357.

21. http://www.nytimes.com/2008/11/05/opinion/05iht -edfriedman.1.17547323.html?_r=0.

22. http://www.civilrights.org/publications/hatecrimes /white-supremacist.html.

23. http://www.cnn.com/2009/US/02/26/hate.groups.report /index.html.

24. http://www.npr.org/templates/story/story.php ?storyId=120715771.

25. Issue Evolution: Race and Transformation of American Politics, Edward Carmines and James Stimson, Princeton University Press, 1989, page 62.

26. In election years these questions were frequently prefaced with: "Between now and the time of the convention in (month) there will be more discussion about the qualifications of presidential candidates – their education, age, religion, race, and the like…"

27. http://www.uky.edu/AS/PoliSci/Peffley/pdf /PeffleyHurwitz%201998%20WHITES%20 STEREOTYPES%20OF%20BLACKS.pdf.

28. http://www.census.gov/newsroom/releases/archives /population/cb12-243.html.

29. http://www.census.gov/newsroom/releases/archives /population/cb12-90.html.

30. http://www.usatoday.com/story/onpolitics/2014/01/20 /sarah-palin-obama-race-mlk-dream-speech/4665031/.

31. http://www.nytimes.com/2010/07/19/opinion /19douthat.html.

32. http://www.salon.com/2016/06/12/donald_trumps _backward_legal_logic_his_recusal_policy_is_reckless _and_incoherent/.

33. http://www.huffingtonpost.com/2008/10/15/rush -limbaugh-blacks-trai_n_134816.html.

34. https://www.youtube.com/watch?v=6NL2qIZbmMo.

35. https://www.youtube.com/watch?v=FiZFzh62noU.

36. https://www.youtube.com/watch?v=oJLZUSRJwJI.

37. http://www.dailykos.com/story/2015/06/21/1394467 /-After-Charleston-the-time-has-come-for-Republicans -to-denounce-hate-peddlers-or-be-stained-by- them?showAll=yes#.

38. Section One. Neither slavery nor involuntary servitude, except as a punishment for crime whereof the party shall have been duly convicted, shall exist within the United States, or any place subject to their jurisdiction. Section Two. Congress shall have power to enforce this article by appropriate legislation.

39. Section 1. All persons born or naturalized in the United
    States, and subject to the jurisdiction thereof, are citizens
    of the United States and of the state wherein they reside.
    No state shall make or enforce any law which shall abridge
    the privileges or immunities of citizens of the United
    States; nor shall any state deprive any person of life, liberty,
    or property, without due process of law; nor deny to any
    person within its jurisdiction the equal protection of the
    laws. Section 2. Representatives shall be apportioned
    among the several states according to their respective
    numbers, counting the whole number of persons in each
    state, excluding Indians not taxed. But when the right to
    vote at any election for the choice of electors for President
    and Vice President of the United States, Representatives
    in Congress, the executive and judicial officers of a state,
    or the members of the legislature thereof, is denied to any
    of the male inhabitants of such state, being twenty-one
    years of age, and citizens of the United States, or in any
    way abridged, except for participation in rebellion, or other
    crime, the basis of representation therein shall be reduced
    in the proportion which the number of such male citizens
    shall bear to the whole number of male citizens twenty-
    one years of age in such state. Section 3. No person shall
    be a Senator or Representative in Congress, or elector of
    President and Vice President, or hold any office, civil or
    military, under the United States, or under any state, who,
    having previously taken an oath, as a member of Congress,
    or as an officer of the United States, or as a member of
    any state legislature, or as an executive or judicial officer
    of any state, to support the Constitution of the United
    States, shall have engaged in insurrection or rebellion
    against the same, or given aid or comfort to the enemies
    thereof. But Congress may by a vote of two-thirds of each
    House, remove such disability. Section 4. The validity
    of the public debt of the United States, authorized by
    law, including debts incurred for payment of pensions
    and bounties for services in suppressing insurrection
    or rebellion, shall not be questioned. But neither the
    United States nor any state shall assume or pay any debt
    or obligation incurred in aid of insurrection or rebellion

against the United States, or any claim for the loss or emancipation of any slave; but all such debts, obligations and claims shall be held illegal and void. Section 5. The Congress shall have power to enforce, by appropriate legislation, the provisions of this article.

40. Section 1.The right of citizens of the United States to vote shall not be denied or abridged by the United States or by any State on account of race, color, or previous condition of servitude. Section. 2 The Congress shall have power to enforce this article by appropriate legislation.

41. http://www.history.com/topics/black-history/rosa-parks.

42. At the cloture vote to end the filibuster against the 1964 Civil Rights Act, Dirksen remarked, "Victor Hugo wrote in his diary substantially this sentiment: 'Stronger than all the armies is an idea whose time has come.' The time has come for equality of opportunity in sharing of government, in education, and in employment. It must not be stayed or denied."

43. *The Southern Strategy Revisited*, Joseph Aistrup, University Press of Kentucky, 1996.

44. "That old time Southern Strategy," Jack Bass, March 24, 2004. <*http://www.salon.com/2004/03/25/southern_strategy/*>.

45. "Nixon's Southern Strategy 'It's All In the Charts'," James Boyd, *New York Times*, May 17, 1970. <http://www.nytimes.com/packages/html/books/phillips-southern.pdf>.

46. Ibid.

47. *The Southern Strategy Revisited*, Joseph Aistrup, University Press of Kentucky, 1996.

48. Ibid.

49. Ibid.

50. Ibid.

51. Ibid.

52. Ibid.

53. Ibid.

54. https://www.youtube.com/watch?v=Io9KMSSEZoY

55. http://articles.chicagotribune.com/1991-10-29
    /news/9104070390_1_rep-david-duke-civil-rights-senate
    -democrats.

56. *The Southern Strategy Revisited*, Joseph Aistrup, University
    Press of Kentucky, 1996.

57. http://www.nytimes.com/1992/11/05/us/1992-elections
    -disappointment-analysis-eccentric-but-no-joke-perot-s
    -strong.html.

58. "South Carolina Debate Fact Check," Robert Pear, *New
    York Times*, January 16, 2012. <*http://thecaucus.blogs.nytimes.
    com/2012/01/16/south-carolina-debate-fact-check/*>.

59. "The end of a long, ugly road for the GOP's Southern
    strategy," Melinda Henneberger, *Washington Post*,
    November 8, 2012. < *http://www.washingtonpost.com/blogs
    /she-the-people/wp/2012/11/08/the-end-of-a-long-ugly-road-for-the
    -gops-southern-strategy/*>

60. "RNC Chief to Say It Was 'Wrong' to Exploit Racial
    Conflict for Votes," Allen Mack, *Washington Post*, July 14,
    2005. <*http://www.washingtonpost.com/wp-dyn/content
    /article/2005/07/13/AR2005071302342.html*>

61. http://climate.nasa.gov/scientific-consensus/.

62. http://www.businessinsider.com/10-percent-of
    -republicans-think-climate-change-is-human-caused-2015-7.

63. http://www.theguardian.com/environment/climate
    -consensus-97-per-cent/2013/aug/08/global-warming
    -denial-fox-news.

64. http://www.pbs.org/wnet/need-to-know/the-daily-need
    /house-republicans-now-officially-on-record-denying
    -science-behind-climate-change/7980/.

65. http://www.theatlantic.com/technology/archive/2010/10
    /why-republicans-deny-climate-change/343790/.

66. Ibid.

67. http://www.washingtonpost.com/r/2010-2019
    /WashingtonPost/2013/10/21/Editorial-Opinion
    /Graphics/E-M10989a-h.pdf.

68. http://unesdoc.unesco.org/images/0012/001282
    /128291eo.pdf.

69. http://www.aaanet.org/stmts/racepp.htm.

70. http://www.thedailybeast.com/articles/2015/06/09/nobel
    -prize-winning-biologist-calls-women-love-hungry-cry
    -babies.html.

71. http://www.huffingtonpost.com/2013/06/05/donald
    -trump-blames-crime_n_3392535.html.

72. http://fair.org/blog/2013/04/25/bill-oreillys-dangerous
    -islamophobia/.

73. http://www.jfklibrary.org/JFK/JFK-in-History/JFK-and
    -Religion.aspx.

74. http://americamagazine.org/node/145218.

75. http://theislamicmonthly.com/the-othering-of-muslim
    -americans/.

76. http://mediamatters.org/research/2006/11/08/matthews
    -some-men-say-sen-clintons-voice-sounds/137264.

77. https://www.youtube.com/watch?v=PKNLIoWyVxo.

78. http://www.debbieschlussel.com/2750/barack-hussein
    -obama-once-a-muslim-always-a-muslim/.

79. http://mediamatters.org/research/2007/01/26/cnn-nbc
    -blame-obama-opponents-for-smears-advanc/137863.

80. Ibid.

81. Ibid.

82. http://www.foxnews.com/story/2007/01/22/hillary
    -clinton-drops-madrassa-bomb-on-barack-obama.html.

83. The United States Constitution, Article VI, paragraph
    3: The Senators and Representatives before mentioned,
    and the Members of the several State Legislatures, and
    all executive and judicial Officers, both of the United
    States and of the several States, shall be bound by Oath or
    Affirmation, to support this Constitution; but no religious
    test shall ever be required as a qualification to any office or
    public trust under the United States.

84. http://mediamatters.org/research/2007/01/26/cnn-nbc
    -blame-obama-opponents-for-smears-advanc/137863.

85. https://www.youtube.com/watch?v=yswEJ8ihnWA.

86. http://www.bls.gov/opub/uscs/1934-36.pdf.

87. According to Forbes magazine, in 2011, the median
    white household had $111,146 in wealth holdings; the
    median Black household $7,113, and the median Hispanic
    household $8,348. http://www.forbes.com/sites
    /laurashin/2015/03/26/the-racial-wealth-gap-why-a-typical
    -white-household-has-16-times-the-wealth-of-a-black
    -one/#568498446c5b.

88. The Color of Welfare: How Racism Undermined the War on
    Poverty, Jill Quadagno, Oxford University Press, 1994.

89. Though according to Thomas Piketty, Capital in the 21st
    Century, this could be changing due to the consolidation of
    wealth; http://www.economist.com/blogs
    /buttonwood/2014/03/inequality.

90. https://www.washingtonpost.com/news/wonk
/wp/2015/05/28/evidence-that-banks-still-deny-black
-borrowers-just-as-they-did-50-years-ago/.

91. http://www.salon.com/2016/07/03/gop_convention
_madness_is_cleveland_ready_for_its_close_up/.

92. http://www.wesh.com/news/man-accused-of-making
-racial-slurs-to-two-children/26944448.

93. http://www.cnn.com/2016/02/12/us/texas-am-racial
-incident/index.html.

94. http://www.politifact.com/punditfact/statements/2015
/mar/15/jalen-ross/black-name-resume-50-percent-less
-likely-get-respo/.

95. http://soletstalkabout.com/post/20999487845/nyc-stop
-and-frisk-statistics.

96. http://www.bjs.gov/index.cfm?ty=tp&tid=702.

97. http://www.drugandalcoholdependence.com/article
/S0376-8716(15)00049-6/abstract.

98. http://www.vocativ.com/underworld/drugs/crack-vs-coke
-sentencing/.

99. Ibid.

100. http://www.cnn.com/2016/03/23/politics/john
-ehrlichman-richard-nixon-drug-war-blacks-hippie
/index.html.

101. https://www.bop.gov/resources/research_projects
/published_reports/pub_vs_priv/oreprcg2000.pdf.

102. http://www.naacp.org/pages/criminal-justice-fact-sheet.

103. Ibid.

104. https://www.propublica.org/article/machine-bias-risk
-assessments-in-criminal-sentencing.

105. http://www.thespectrum.com/story/news/nation
-now/2014/08/15/data-white-cops-kill-black-people
-week/14151677/.

106. http://www.huffingtonpost.com/2012/05/03/racial-bias
-doctors_n_1472281.html.

107. http://www.medicalnewstoday.com/releases/242975.php.

108. Ibid.

109. http://blacklivesmatter.com/guiding-principles/.

110. Ibid.

111. http://www.huffingtonpost.com/entry/bill-oreilly-black
-lives-matter_us_57465f7ee4b055bb1171385f.

112. http://www.nytimes.com/2014/04/24/us/politics
/rancher-proudly-breaks-the-law-becoming-a-hero-in-the
-west.html?_r=0.

113. https://www.youtube.com/watch?v=Of7FWFkhidM.

114. http://www.motherjones.com/politics/2014/08/ferguson
-st-louis-police-tactics-dogs-michael-brown.

115. Ibid.

116. Ibid.

117. https://www.youtube.com/watch?v=DoYwJic4QTs.

118. http://video.foxnews.com/v/3741094028001/the-truth
-about-ferguson/?#sp=show-clips.

119. http://www.nytimes.com/2012/08/20/us/politics/todd
-akin-provokes-ire-with-legitimate-rape-comment.html
?_r=0.

120. http://uproxx.com/news/brock-turner-judge-harsh
-sentence-immigrant/.

121. http://www.huffingtonpost.com/2012/03/23/geraldo
-rivera-trayvon-martin-hoodie_n_1375080.html.

122. http://www.theatlantic.com/magazine/archive/2011/09
/the-secret-history-of-guns/308608/.

123. http://www.huffingtonpost.com/entry/falcon-heights
-shooting_us_577dd795e4b0c590f7e8058f.

124. http://www.diversityinc.com/news/study-seeing
-successful-black-people-makes-non-blacks-deny-racism/.

125. https://www.census.gov/hhes/socdemo/education/data
/census/half-century/tables.html

126. https://www.youtube.com/watch?v=MRq6Y4NmB6U.

127. https://www.youtube.com/watch?v=-evDW3sJddQ.

128. https://www.dailymotion.com/video/x6zudi_sarah-palin
-special-comment_news.

129. http://ropercenter.cornell.edu/polls/us-elections/how
-groups-voted/how-groups-voted-2008/.

130. http://ropercenter.cornell.edu/polls/us-elections/how
-groups-voted/how-groups-voted-2012/.

131. https://www.washingtonpost.com/news/wonk/
wp/2014/08/06/a-comprehensive-investigation-of-voter
-impersonation-finds-31-credible-incidents-out-of-one
-billion-ballots-cast/.

132. http://www.rollingstone.com/politics/news/how
-republicans-rig-the-game-20131111.

133. http://talkingpointsmemo.com/muckraker/pennsylvania
-gop-leader-voter-id-will-help-romney-win-state.

134. "Prejudice and Politics: Symbolic Racism Versus Racial
Threats to the Good Life," David R. Kinder and David O.
Sears, *Journal of Personality and Social Psychology,* 1981, Vol.
40, No. 3, 414-431.

135. "Why Do White Americans Oppose Race-Targeted Policies? Clarifying the Impact of Symbolic Racism", Rabinowitz, et.al., 2009.

136. "Racism, Ideology, and Affirmative Action Revisited: The Antecedents and Consequences of 'Principled Objections' to Affirmative Action," Christopher M. Federico, Jim Sidanius, *Journal of Personality and Social Psychology*, 2002, Vol. 82, No. 4, 488-502.

137. "Symbolic Racism: Problems of Motive Attribution in Political Analysis," Paul M. Sniderman, Philip E. Tetlock, 1986, *Journal of Social Issues*, Vol. 42, 2, 129-50.

138. http://condor.depaul.edu/phenry1/SR2Kinstructions.htm.

139. *Divided by Color: Racial Politics and Democratic Ideals*, Donald R. Kinder and Lynn M. Sanders, University of Chicago Press, 1996.

140. "The Structure of White Racial Attitudes," Stanley Feldman and Leonine Huddy, 2010.

141. "Explaining the Great Racial Divide: Perceptions of Fairness in the U.S. Criminal Justice System," Jon Hurwitz and Mark Peffley, *The Journal of Politics*, Vol. 67, No. 3, 762–783, 2005.

142. "Racial Prejudice and Fears of Criminal Victimization by Strangers in Public Settings," Craig St. John and Tamara Heald-Moore, *Sociological Inquiry*, Vol. 66, No. 3, 267–284, 1996.

143. Multiple regression analyses (ordered logistic) conducted on each public figure while controlling for both voter party identification and ideology support these results.

144. "Seeking Unity, Obama Feels Pull of Racial Divide," Ginger Thompson; Jeff Zeleny and Kitty Bennett contributed reporting, *The New York Times*, 12 February 2008.

145. "Obama Puts Race Closer To Center Of Campaign," Jackie Calmes and Nick Timiraos, *The Wall Street Journal*, March 19, 2008.

146. http://www.nationalreview.com/article/223982/justifying-scandalous-dereliction-charles-krauthammer.

147. http://www.nydailynews.com/news/politics/barack-obama-shows-amazing-grace-article-1.286599.

148. "Obama Puts Race Closer To Center Of Campaign," Jackie Calmes and Nick Timiraos, *The Wall Street Journal*, March 19, 2008.

149. My italics.

150. My italics.

151. Ordinal regression models of each candidate's favorable ratings support these findings—racial antagonism affecting views of Obama but not McCain—even when concurrently controlling for partisan effects.

152. "Racial stereotypes of one hundred college students," D. Katz and K. Braly, *Journal of Abnormal and Social Psychology*, 28, 280–290, 1933.

153. Potentially positive (or at least not pejorative) stereotypes included that "negroes" were "very religious" and "musical."

154. "Are Racial Stereotypes Really Fading? The Princeton Trilogy Revisited," Patricia G. Devine and Andrew J. Elliot, *Personality and Social Psychology Bulletin*, Vol 21, 11, 1139–50, 1995.

155. Survey by Cable News Network. Methodology: Conducted by Opinion Research Corporation, March 14–March 16, 2008 and based on 1,019 telephone interviews.

156. "A Model of (Often Mixed) Stereotype Content: Competence and Warmth Respectively Follow From Perceived Status and Competition," Fiske, et al, *Journal of Personality and Social Psychology*, Vol. 82, 6, 878–902, 2002.

157. "The Meaning of Stereotypes", James W. Rinehart, 1963, http://eric.ed.gov/?id=ED002565.

158. http://www.rollingstone.com/politics/news/republicans
-are-huge-hypocrites-about-merrick-garland-20160321.

159. http://www.npr.org/templates/story/story.
php?storyId=121158951.

160. http://money.cnn.com/2011/08/05/news/economy
/downgrade_rumors/index.htm.

161. http://www.economist.com/node/21525905.

162. http://www.nytimes.com/2015/03/10/world/asia/white
-house-faults-gop-senators-letter-to-irans-leaders.html.

163. http://www.nytimes.com/2012/02/15/health/policy/
health-care-mandate-was-first-backed-by-conservatives.
html.

164. https://www.eisenhower.archives.gov/research/online
_documents/interstate_highway_system.html.

165. https://thinkprogress.org/mitch-mcconnell-i-want-to-be
-senate-majority-leader-in-order-to-make-obama-a-one
-term-president-6645c279b275#.vts7407ts.

166. http://thinkprogress.org/politics/2009/01/20/35012
/limbaugh-obama-fail/.

167. https://www.washingtonpost.com/blogs/plum-line
/wp/2016/09/12/the-american-people-agree-with-clinton
-trump-is-a-bigot-this-new-poll-confirms-it/?postshare=32
21473769743881&tid=ss_tw&utm_term=.370c1864f137.

168. https://www.youtube.com/watch?v=wcPGiGvo-uU.

169. Lyric from "Mary Don't You Weep," what scholars call
a "slave song," originating before the Civil War and
containing coded messages of resistance and hope. It is one
of the most important of Negro spirituals.

170. http://nymag.com/daily/intelligencer/2016/09/lauers
-pathetic-interview-made-me-think-trump-can-win.html.

171. http://www.nytimes.com/2016/09/20/public-editor /trump-birther-lie-liz-spayd-public-editor.html?_r=0.

172. http://www.politifact.com/personalities/donald-trump/.

173. http://abcnews.go.com/Politics/donald-trump-lets-jimmy -fallon-mess-hair/story?id=42127031.

174. http://thegrio.com/2016/09/21/john-lewis-wants-feds-at -polling-election-day/.

175. https://www.washingtonpost.com/news/worldviews /wp/2015/08/13/germany-won-respect-by-addressing-its -world-war-ii-crimes-japan-not-so-much/.

176. Acts 3:19

177. Luke 13:3